What Humans Should Learn From Donkeys?

HB Goldsmith

Preface

In the hurried pace of modern life, where the clamor of technology often drowns out the whispers of nature, it's easy to overlook the profound wisdom that surrounds us in the most unexpected places. Among the bucolic landscapes and dusty trails, amidst the rhythmic clip-clop of hooves, there exists a creature whose quiet presence belies a wealth of insight—the donkey.

As I reflect on my own encounters with these humble beings, I am struck by the depth of wisdom they possess and the invaluable lessons they offer to humanity. It is this realization that has inspired me to embark on a journey of exploration—a journey to uncover the hidden treasures of donkey wisdom and share them with the world.

In the pages of this book, **What Humans Should Learn From Donkeys?**, we will venture into the world of donkeys, not merely as beasts of burden, but as teachers and guides. We will delve into their rich history, tracing their footsteps through the annals of time, and discover the profound impact they have had on human civilization.

But more than a historical account, this book is a celebration of the timeless virtues embodied by donkeys—virtues such as patience, humility, and resilience. Through poignant anecdotes, insightful observations, and practical advice, we will explore how these virtues can enrich our own lives and guide us on the path to greater fulfillment and purpose.

Drawing on personal experiences as well as the wisdom of experts and scholars, we will journey through the rolling hills of rural landscapes and the bustling streets of urban jungles, seeking out the echoes of donkey wisdom that reverberate through our world.

It is my sincere hope that this book will serve as a beacon of inspiration for all who read it—a reminder to slow down, listen closely, and embrace the wisdom that surrounds us in its simplest, most unassuming forms. May it awaken within you a newfound appreciation for the gentle creatures who share our planet and a deeper understanding of the profound lessons they have to teach us.

So, as we embark on this journey together, let us open our hearts and minds to the wisdom of the donkey, and may we emerge enriched, enlightened, and inspired to live our lives with greater compassion, authenticity, and purpose.

About Author

HB Goldsmith (Dr. Hiren B. Soni) is an avid animal lover, philosopher, and writer dedicated to exploring the wisdom of the natural world and its relevance to human life. With a background in educational psychology, bird and animal behavior, and a passion for understanding the intricacies of human behavior, Goldsmith has spent 26 years studying the behavior of animals, including the often-overlooked donkey.

Inspired by the quiet strength and gentle demeanor of this noble creature, Goldsmith embarked on a journey to uncover the profound lessons that donkeys can teach us about resilience, compassion, and living in harmony with nature. Drawing from personal experiences and extensive research, Goldsmith crafted "**What Humans Should Learn from Donkeys**" as a guidebook for personal growth and transformation.

In addition to writing, Goldsmith is also a sought-after writer and mentoring facilitator, sharing insights from the book with audiences around the State as well as Country. Through engaging storytelling and thought-provoking discussions, Goldsmith inspires others to embrace the wisdom of donkeys and live more fulfilling, compassionate lives.

When not writing or speaking, Goldsmith can often be found exploring the great outdoors, communing with nature, and spending time with beloved animal companions. With a deep reverence for the natural world and a commitment to living in alignment with its principles, Goldsmith continues to spread the message of donkey wisdom and its transformative power to audiences everywhere.

Table of Contents

Prologue 10

Chapter 1: The Wisdom of Patience 12

   - Understanding the Donkey's Enduring Patience 14

   - Applying Patience in Human Life: Lessons from the Donkey 16

Chapter 2: Embracing Humility 19

   - Humble Beginnings: The Donkey's Role Throughout History 21

   - Humility in Action: How Donkeys Teach Us to Stay Grounded 23

Chapter 3: Strength in Serenity 26

   - The Quiet Strength of Donkeys: A Lesson in Serenity 28

   - Finding Inner Strength through Calmness and Contentment 30

Chapter 4: The Power of Listening 33

   - Tuning into the Silent Wisdom of Donkeys 35

   - Enhancing Communication through Active Listening 37

Chapter 5: Finding Joy in the Simple Things 40

   - Donkeys and Delight: Embracing Life's Simple Pleasures 42

   - Cultivating Joy Amidst Life's Challenges 44

Chapter 6: Endurance Through Adversity 47

   - Tales of Resilience: How Donkeys Persevere 49

- Building Resilience in the Face of Obstacles 51

Chapter 7: Navigating Life's Trails with Grace 54

- Grace Under Pressure: Lessons in Gracefulness from Donkeys 55

- Maintaining Gracefulness Through Life's Twists and Turns 57

Chapter 8: Loyalty and Trust 60

- Loyalty Unbridled: The Donkey's Unwavering Commitment 62

- Nurturing Trust and Loyalty in Human Relationships 64

Chapter 9: The Art of Self-Preservation 67

- Survival Instincts: Donkeys and the Art of Self-Preservation 69

- Balancing Self-Care and Care for Others 71

Chapter 10: Respect for Boundaries 74

- Honoring Space: Understanding Donkey Boundaries 76

- Establishing Healthy Boundaries for Personal Well-being 78

Chapter 11: The Language of Body and Soul 81

- Unspoken Communication: Deciphering Donkey Body Language 83

- Deepening Connections Through Nonverbal Communication 85

Chapter 12: Leading with Gentle Guidance 88

- Leading with Love: Donkeys as Gentle Leaders 90

- Harnessing the Power of Compassionate Leadership 92

Chapter 13: Community and Cooperation 95

- The Strength of Herds: Donkeys and the Importance of Community 97

- Fostering Collaboration and Cooperation in Human Society 100

Chapter 14: Facing Challenges Head-On 103

- Boldly Confronting Challenges: Lessons from Donkey Behavior 105

- Building Courage and Tenacity in the Face of Adversity 107

Chapter 15: Resilience in the Face of Criticism 110

- Thick Skin and Tender Hearts: Donkeys and Dealing with Criticism 112

- Developing Resilience in Times of Judgment and Doubt 115

Chapter 16: Living in Harmony with Nature 118

- Donkeys and the Rhythms of Nature: A Lesson in Harmony 120

- Cultivating Eco-consciousness and Sustainability 123

Chapter 17: Embracing Individuality 126

- Celebrating Uniqueness: Donkeys and the Beauty of Diversity 128

- Embracing Individuality and Authenticity in Human Life 131

Chapter 18: The Gift of Contentment 134

- Contentment in Stillness: Donkeys and the Art of Being Present 136

- Finding Fulfillment in the Here and Now 138

Chapter 19: Lessons in Forgiveness and Compassion 142

- Forgiveness Unbridled: Donkeys and the Power of Letting Go 144

- Cultivating Forgiveness and Compassion in Human Relationships 147

Chapter 20: Cultivating Gratitude and Appreciation .. 151

- Grateful Hearts: Donkeys and the Practice of Appreciation 153

- Nurturing Gratitude for Life's Blessings 156

Conclusion 160

Epilogue 162

Glossary 164

Bibliography 168

Prologue

In the vast tapestry of life, there are moments of stillness, whispers amidst the cacophony of existence, where profound truths reveal themselves in the most unassuming of forms. Such moments are often found in the company of creatures who inhabit the quiet corners of our world, creatures like the donkey. Picture, if you will, a sun-drenched meadow, where the grass sways gently in the breeze and the air is filled with the sweet scent of wildflowers. Amidst this idyllic scene stands a lone figure—a donkey, his ears perked forward inquisitively, his eyes reflecting a depth of wisdom that transcends mere words.

For centuries, the donkey has been a steadfast companion to humanity, serving as a loyal friend, a tireless worker, and a silent witness to the ebb and flow of human history. From the dusty roads of ancient civilizations to the modern-day countryside, the donkey has walked alongside us, leaving indelible footprints upon the sands of time. But beyond their role as beasts of burden, donkeys possess a quiet grace and dignity that speak to something deeper—a wisdom born of simplicity, resilience, and an unwavering connection to the rhythms of nature. It is this wisdom that beckons us to pause, to listen, and to learn.

In the pages that follow, we will embark on a journey into the heart of donkey wisdom—a journey that will take us through the rolling hills of pastoral landscapes, the bustling markets of ancient cities, and the quietude of the stable. Along the way, we will encounter tales of perseverance, humility, and the timeless truths that lie at the core of the donkey's being. Through stories, anecdotes, and reflections, we will uncover the profound lessons that donkeys have to offer us—lessons that speak to the very essence of what it means to be human. From the importance of patience and humility to the power of resilience and compassion, we will discover how these gentle creatures can guide us on our own journey towards greater understanding, connection, and fulfillment.

So, dear reader, as we embark on this voyage of discovery together, let us open our hearts and minds to the wisdom of the donkey, and may we emerge transformed, inspired, and enriched by the lessons they have to teach us. For in the quiet presence of the donkey, we may just find the keys to unlocking the mysteries of our own hearts and the wisdom to navigate the journey of life with grace, humility, and an open heart.

Welcome to the world of donkey wisdom—where ears are always forward, and hearts are forever open.

Chapter 1: The Wisdom of Patience

In a world that often glorifies speed, efficiency, and instant results, the virtue of patience may seem like a relic of a bygone era. Yet, in the tranquil presence of the humble donkey, we find a timeless reminder of the profound power and wisdom that patience holds.

Understanding the Donkey's Enduring Patience

Imagine a pastoral scene bathed in the golden hues of dawn, where donkeys graze leisurely in the meadow, their movements measured and deliberate. Here, amidst the symphony of nature's rhythms, the donkey stands as a paragon of patience, embodying a calmness that seems to transcend time itself.

Donkeys have long been revered for their stoic patience, a quality honed over centuries of coexistence with humans and the natural world. Whether patiently waiting for their turn at the watering hole or pulling heavy loads under the scorching sun, these gentle creatures demonstrate an unwavering resolve and acceptance of the present moment.

But the donkey's patience extends far beyond mere endurance; it is a profound acceptance of the ebb and flow of life, a willingness to trust in the unfolding of events without resistance or haste. It is this deep-rooted sense of patience that allows donkeys to navigate life's trials with grace and resilience, inspiring awe and admiration in all who observe them.

Applying Patience in Human Life: Lessons from the Donkey

In a world driven by instant gratification and constant stimulation, the wisdom of the donkey offers a much-needed antidote to the frenetic pace of modern life. By observing the donkey's patient demeanor and steadfast resolve, we can learn to cultivate a deeper sense of inner calm and serenity in our own lives.

Patience, as exemplified by the donkey, is not merely a passive state of waiting; it is an active practice—a conscious choice to embrace the present moment with openness and acceptance. It is through patience that we learn to relinquish our attachment to outcomes and surrender to the flow of life, trusting that all things will unfold in their own time.

Moreover, the donkey teaches us that patience is not a sign of weakness, but rather a source of strength and resilience. It is through patient perseverance that we develop the resilience and fortitude to weather life's storms with grace and dignity, emerging stronger and wiser on the other side.

As we journey through the complexities of human existence, let us heed the gentle teachings of the donkey and embrace the power of patience in our own lives. For in the quiet moments of waiting, we may just discover the profound beauty and richness of the present moment, and the timeless wisdom that lies within.

- Understanding the Donkey's Enduring Patience

At the heart of every donkey's demeanor lies an unwavering sense of patience—a virtue that seems to flow effortlessly through their very being. To comprehend the depth of this enduring patience, one must delve into the essence of the donkey's nature and the environment in which they thrive.

1. Embracing the Rhythms of Nature: Donkeys are creatures deeply attuned to the natural world around them. From the rising of the sun to the setting of the moon, they move through life with an innate understanding of the cyclical patterns that govern the universe. In their patient observance of nature's rhythms, donkeys embody a profound acceptance of the ebb and flow of life, embracing each moment with grace and equanimity.

2. Resilience in the Face of Adversity: Life for a donkey is not always easy. From carrying heavy burdens to enduring harsh weather conditions, they face a myriad of challenges with stoic perseverance. Yet, despite the hardships they encounter, donkeys do not falter. Instead, they draw upon their reserves of patience to navigate through adversity, emerging stronger and more resilient with each trial they overcome.

3. Trust in the Process: One of the most remarkable aspects of a donkey's patience is their unwavering trust in the process of life. Whether waiting patiently for their turn at the feeding trough or standing calmly while being groomed, donkeys approach each moment with a sense of trust and surrender. They understand that all things come in their own time, and they have faith in the natural order of things.

4. Cultivating Inner Peace: In the serene presence of a donkey, there is a palpable sense of tranquility—a tranquility born of patience and inner peace. Donkeys do not rush or fret; they simply exist in the present moment, fully embracing the beauty and simplicity of life. In their quiet demeanor, they remind us of the importance of slowing down, of taking a moment to breathe and savor the richness of each passing moment.

5. Leading by Example: Perhaps the most profound aspect of a donkey's enduring patience is their ability to lead by example. Through their actions, they teach us the value of patience, resilience, and trust—virtues that are increasingly rare in our fast-paced world. In the presence of a donkey, we are reminded of the beauty and wisdom that can be found in simply being, and we are inspired to cultivate these virtues in our own lives.

The enduring patience of the donkey serves as a beacon of light in a world consumed by haste and urgency. It is a reminder that true strength lies not in rushing forward, but in standing still—in embracing the present moment with openness and acceptance, and in trusting in the timeless rhythms of life.

- Applying Patience in Human Life: Lessons from the Donkey

The donkey's enduring patience serves as a profound source of inspiration and guidance for humanity, offering invaluable lessons on how we can cultivate this virtue in our own lives. By observing the donkey's patient demeanor and steadfast resolve, we can glean insights into how we can navigate the complexities of human existence with grace and resilience.

1. Cultivating Inner Calmness: In a world characterized by constant noise and distraction, the donkey teaches us the importance of cultivating inner calmness and tranquility. By practicing patience, we can learn to quiet the restless chatter of our minds and find peace amidst the chaos, allowing us to approach life's challenges with a sense of clarity and equanimity.

2. Trusting the Process: Much like the donkey, we can learn to trust in the process of life and surrender to the natural flow of events. Instead of constantly striving to control outcomes and force our will upon the world, we can adopt a more patient and accepting attitude, trusting that everything will unfold in its own time and according to a higher plan.

3. Building Resilience and Fortitude: Patience is not merely a passive state of waiting; it is an active practice that requires strength and resilience. By embracing patience, we can develop the fortitude to persevere in the face of adversity and overcome life's obstacles with grace and dignity. Like the donkey, we can draw upon our inner reserves of patience to weather the storms of life and emerge stronger and more resilient than ever before.

4. Embracing the Present Moment: The donkey's patient demeanor reminds us of the importance of being fully present in each moment and savoring the richness of life as it unfolds. Instead of constantly rushing ahead to the next task or goal, we can learn to slow down and appreciate the beauty and simplicity of the present moment, finding joy and fulfillment in the here and now.

5. Leading by Example: As we cultivate patience in our own lives, we have the opportunity to lead by example and inspire others to do the same. By embodying the virtues of patience, resilience, and trust, we can create a ripple effect of positivity and transformation, spreading peace and harmony throughout our communities and the world at large.

The lessons of patience gleaned from the donkey are timeless and universal, offering profound insights into how we can live more fulfilling, meaningful lives. By embracing the wisdom of the donkey and applying it to our own lives, we can cultivate a deeper sense of peace, resilience, and joy, transforming ourselves and the world around us in the process.

Chapter 2: Embracing Humility

In a world often characterized by ego, ambition, and the relentless pursuit of status, the virtue of humility shines like a beacon of light—a reminder of the inherent dignity and worth of all beings. In this chapter, we will explore the profound wisdom of the donkey as a paragon of humility, offering lessons on how we can embrace this noble virtue in our own lives.

1. Humble Beginnings: The donkey's journey begins in the humblest of circumstances—a creature of the earth, born into a world of simplicity and quiet dignity. From the moment of their birth, donkeys embody the essence of humility, moving through life with a quiet grace and unassuming presence that belies their innate strength and resilience.

2. Serving without Seeking Recognition: One of the most remarkable aspects of the donkey's humility is their willingness to serve without seeking recognition or reward. Whether pulling a plow in the fields or carrying burdens along dusty roads, donkeys perform their tasks with quiet dedication and selflessness, content to simply do their part without expectation of praise or accolades.

3. Standing Firm in the Face of Adversity: Despite their unassuming nature, donkeys possess a quiet strength and resilience that is born of humility. When faced with challenges or obstacles, they do not boast or brag; rather, they stand firm with quiet resolve, drawing upon their inner reserves of strength and fortitude to persevere in the face of adversity.

4. Embracing Equality and Unity: In the presence of a donkey, there is a palpable sense of equality and unity—a recognition of the inherent worth and dignity of all beings. Donkeys do not judge others based on their status or wealth; rather, they treat all creatures with kindness and respect, embodying the timeless wisdom that true greatness lies not in elevating oneself above others, but in lifting others up with humility and compassion.

5. Learning from Nature's Wisdom: Finally, the donkey teaches us to look to the natural world for guidance and inspiration. In the quiet beauty of a sunlit meadow or the rugged terrain of a mountain trail, we find echoes of the donkey's humility—a reminder that true wisdom lies not in the grandeur of our achievements, but in the simple act of being, and in the quiet humility that comes from walking gently upon the earth.

The donkey's humility serves as a powerful reminder of the importance of humility in our own lives. By embracing the virtues of simplicity, selflessness, and quiet strength embodied by the donkey, we can cultivate a deeper sense of humility and grace, enriching our own lives and the lives of those around us in the process.

- Humble Beginnings: The Donkey's Role Throughout History

The donkey's journey through history is one of quiet humility, yet its impact on human civilization has been profound and far-reaching. From its humble beginnings as a beast of burden to its enduring presence in cultures around the world, the donkey has played a vital role in shaping the course of human history.

1. Companion of Civilization: For millennia, the donkey has been a faithful companion to humanity, serving as a reliable workhorse in agricultural societies and a trusted mode of transportation in ancient civilizations. From the fertile valleys of Mesopotamia to the bustling streets of ancient Rome, donkeys were a ubiquitous presence, indispensable to the daily lives of countless people.

2. Symbol of Humility and Service: Throughout history, the donkey has been revered as a symbol of humility and service—a reminder of the value of quiet strength and selflessness. In religious traditions around the world, the donkey is often portrayed as a humble creature, bearing the burdens of humanity with grace and dignity.

3. Unsung Hero of Exploration and Trade: During the age of exploration and trade, donkeys played a crucial role in opening up new frontiers and connecting distant lands. From the Silk Road to the Trans-Saharan trade routes, donkeys carried goods and supplies across vast expanses of desert and mountain terrain, facilitating the exchange of ideas, cultures, and commodities between civilizations.

4. Guardian of Biodiversity: In modern times, the donkey's role has evolved to include conservation efforts aimed at preserving biodiversity and traditional ways of life. In rural communities around the world, donkeys continue to play a vital role in sustainable agriculture, helping to cultivate the land and maintain fragile ecosystems.

5. Enduring Legacy: Despite advances in technology and changes in societal norms, the donkey's legacy endures as a testament to the enduring power of humility and service. From the rolling hills of rural landscapes to the bustling streets of urban centers, the donkey remains a beloved and cherished companion, embodying the timeless virtues that have sustained civilizations for millennia.

The donkey's role throughout history serves as a powerful reminder of the value of humility and service in shaping the course of human civilization. By honoring the humble beginnings of the donkey and the vital role it has played in the journey of humanity, we gain a deeper appreciation for the quiet strength and resilience that lie at the heart of this remarkable creature.

- Humility in Action: How Donkeys Teach Us to Stay Grounded

In the quiet presence of a donkey, there is a profound lesson in humility—a virtue that is often overlooked in a world that celebrates grandiosity and self-promotion. Donkeys embody humility in every aspect of their being, teaching us valuable lessons on how to stay grounded and true to ourselves in the face of life's challenges.

1. Embracing Simplicity: Donkeys lead lives of simplicity, finding contentment in the most basic of pleasures. They do not seek out fame or fortune; rather, they find joy in the simple act of grazing in a sunlit pasture or feeling the gentle caress of a cool breeze. In their humble existence, donkeys remind us of the beauty and richness that can be found in leading a life of simplicity and moderation.

2. Working Quietly Behind the Scenes: One of the most striking aspects of a donkey's humility is their willingness to work quietly behind the scenes, without seeking recognition or praise. Whether plowing fields or carrying burdens, donkeys perform their tasks with quiet dedication and selflessness, content to simply do their part without expectation of reward. In their unassuming service, they teach us the value of humility and the importance of finding fulfillment in the act of giving, rather than receiving.

3. Remaining Grounded in Adversity: Donkeys possess a quiet strength and resilience that is born of humility. When faced with adversity or hardship, they do not boast or brag; rather, they stand firm with quiet resolve, drawing upon their inner reserves of strength and fortitude to persevere in the face of challenges. In their steadfast demeanor, they remind us that true greatness lies not in the absence of struggle, but in the ability to remain grounded and true to ourselves in the midst of adversity.

4. Treating Others with Kindness and Respect: In the presence of a donkey, there is a palpable sense of kindness and respect—a recognition of the inherent worth and dignity of all beings. Donkeys do not judge others based on their status or wealth; rather, they treat all creatures with kindness and compassion, embodying the timeless wisdom that true greatness lies not in elevating oneself above others, but in lifting others up with humility and grace.

5. Leading by Example: Ultimately, the donkey's humility serves as a powerful example for us all—a reminder of the value of humility and service in shaping the course of our lives. By embodying the virtues of simplicity, selflessness, and quiet strength embodied by the donkey, we can cultivate a deeper sense of humility and grace, enriching our own lives and the lives of those around us in the process.

The lessons of humility gleaned from the donkey are timeless and universal, offering profound insights into how we can lead lives of greater meaning and purpose. By embracing the wisdom of the donkey and applying it to our own lives, we can learn to stay grounded and true to ourselves, even in the face of life's greatest challenges.

Chapter 3: Strength in Serenity

In the tranquil presence of a donkey, one cannot help but be struck by the quiet strength and serenity that emanate from these gentle creatures. In this chapter, we will explore the profound wisdom of the donkey as a symbol of serenity, offering lessons on how we can cultivate inner strength and resilience through the practice of tranquility.

1. The Quiet Strength of Donkeys: Donkeys possess a quiet strength that is born of serenity—a steadfast resolve that allows them to navigate life's challenges with grace and equanimity. Whether standing stoically in a sunlit pasture or pulling a heavy load along a dusty road, donkeys exude a sense of calmness and composure that belies their innate power.

2. Finding Peace in Stillness: In the hustle and bustle of modern life, finding moments of stillness can be a rare and precious gift. Yet, donkeys seem to revel in the peace and tranquility of the present moment, finding solace in the simple act of being. In their quiet contemplation, they teach us the importance of slowing down, taking a breath, and finding peace amidst the chaos.

3. Cultivating Inner Resilience: Serenity is not merely a state of relaxation; it is a source of inner strength and resilience. By cultivating a sense of tranquility in our own lives, we can learn to weather life's storms with grace and dignity, drawing upon our inner reserves of strength and fortitude to persevere in the face of adversity.

4. Embracing Acceptance and Letting Go: At the heart of serenity lies a profound acceptance of life as it is—a willingness to let go of attachments and surrender to the flow of existence. Donkeys understand this implicitly, embracing each moment with open arms and an open heart. In their quiet acceptance, they teach us the value of letting go of the need to control outcomes and trusting in the natural order of things.

5. Finding Joy in the Present Moment: Ultimately, the practice of serenity leads us to a deeper sense of joy and fulfillment in the present moment. Like the donkey grazing in a sunlit meadow or basking in the warmth of a summer breeze, we can learn to find beauty and contentment in the simple pleasures of life, savoring each moment with gratitude and appreciation.

The strength of the donkey lies not in brute force or aggression, but in the quiet serenity that comes from being at peace with oneself and the world. By embracing the wisdom of the donkey and cultivating a sense of tranquility in our own lives, we can discover a deeper sense of inner strength and resilience, leading to a life of greater peace, joy, and fulfillment.

- The Quiet Strength of Donkeys: A Lesson in Serenity

At first glance, the donkey may appear unassuming, perhaps even meek. Yet, upon closer inspection, one cannot help but be struck by the profound sense of strength and serenity that emanates from these gentle creatures. In this section, we will explore how the donkey's quiet strength serves as a powerful lesson in the practice of serenity.

1. Stoicism in Stillness: In the serene presence of a donkey, there is a palpable sense of stillness—a quiet calm that pervades the air. Whether standing stoically in a sunlit meadow or gazing out over a vast expanse of countryside, donkeys embody a sense of peace and tranquility that seems to transcend the chaos of the world around them. In their quietude, they teach us the value of finding solace in stillness, and the power of serenity to anchor us amidst life's storms.

2. Resilience in Adversity: Despite their tranquil demeanor, donkeys possess a quiet strength that is born of resilience. When faced with challenges or obstacles, they do not panic or flee; rather, they stand firm with quiet resolve, drawing upon their inner reserves of strength and fortitude to weather the storm. In their steadfastness, they teach us the importance of remaining grounded and centered in the face of adversity, and the power of serenity to sustain us through life's trials.

3. Grace in Action: Donkeys move through life with a grace and elegance that belies their humble appearance. Whether trotting along a dusty trail or grazing in a sun-dappled pasture, they move with a sense of purpose and poise that is both captivating and inspiring. In their graceful movements, they teach us the value of embracing life with dignity and grace, and the power of serenity to infuse even the simplest of actions with beauty and meaning.

4. Trusting in the Flow: At the heart of a donkey's serenity lies a profound trust in the natural order of things. They do not resist or struggle against the currents of life; rather, they surrender to the flow, trusting that all things will unfold as they are meant to. In their trust, they teach us the importance of letting go of the need to control outcomes, and the power of serenity to cultivate a sense of ease and acceptance in our lives.

5. Leading by Example: Ultimately, the donkey's quiet strength serves as a powerful example for us all—a reminder of the value of serenity in navigating the complexities of human existence. By embodying the virtues of stillness, resilience, grace, and trust exemplified by the donkey, we can cultivate a deeper sense of serenity in our own lives, leading to greater peace, joy, and fulfillment.

The quiet strength of the donkey serves as a powerful testament to the transformative power of serenity. By embracing the lessons of stillness, resilience, grace, and trust embodied by the donkey, we can learn to navigate life's challenges with greater ease and grace, and discover a deeper sense of peace and contentment along the way.

- Finding Inner Strength through Calmness and Contentment

In the hustle and bustle of modern life, amidst the constant demands and distractions, finding moments of calmness and contentment can feel like a rare and precious gift. Yet, it is in these moments of serenity that we often discover our greatest reserves of inner strength and resilience. In this section, we will explore how cultivating a sense of calmness and contentment can lead to greater inner strength and fulfillment.

1. Embracing Stillness: In a world filled with noise and chaos, finding moments of stillness can be a profound source of nourishment for the soul. Whether through meditation, mindfulness, or simply taking a quiet walk in nature, carving out time for stillness allows us to reconnect with our inner selves and tap into a deeper reservoir of strength and wisdom.

2. Cultivating Gratitude: Gratitude is a powerful practice that can transform our perception of the world around us. By focusing on the blessings and abundance in our lives, rather than dwelling on what is lacking, we can cultivate a sense of contentment and fulfillment that transcends external circumstances. In this state of gratitude, we discover that true strength lies not in what we possess, but in our ability to appreciate and savor the richness of life.

3. Trusting in the Flow of Life: At the heart of calmness and contentment lies a profound trust in the natural order of things. Instead of resisting or struggling against the currents of life, we learn to surrender and trust that all things will unfold as they are meant to. In this state of trust, we discover a deep sense of peace and acceptance that allows us to navigate life's challenges with grace and resilience.

4. Finding Joy in the Present Moment: Calmness and contentment are not fleeting states of happiness based on external circumstances; rather, they are enduring qualities that arise from within. By learning to be fully present in each moment and savoring the richness of life as it unfolds, we discover a profound sense of joy and fulfillment that transcends the ups and downs of life.

5. Leading by Example: Ultimately, the practice of cultivating calmness and contentment serves as a powerful example for others—a beacon of light in a world often consumed by stress and striving. By embodying the virtues of stillness, gratitude, trust, and presence, we inspire those around us to embrace these qualities in their own lives, leading to greater peace, harmony, and well-being for all.

Finding inner strength through calmness and contentment is not about seeking external validation or striving for perfection; rather, it is about learning to cultivate a sense of peace and fulfillment from within. By embracing the practice of stillness, gratitude, trust, and presence, we can tap into our greatest reservoirs of inner strength and resilience, leading to a life of greater peace, joy, and fulfillment.

Chapter 4: The Power of Listening

In a world filled with noise and chatter, the art of listening is often overlooked and undervalued. Yet, for those who have had the privilege of spending time in the company of a donkey, it becomes abundantly clear that listening is a skill worth cultivating. In this chapter, we will explore the profound wisdom of the donkey as a masterful listener, and the transformative power that lies in the simple act of paying attention.

1. The Language of Silence: Donkeys are creatures of few words, yet their ability to communicate through silence is unparalleled. Whether standing quietly in a field or grazing alongside companions, donkeys possess a keen awareness of their surroundings and an intuitive understanding of the subtle cues and signals that pass between them. In their silent presence, they teach us the value of tuning into the language of silence and listening with an open heart and mind.

2. Honoring the Wisdom of the Herd: In the social hierarchy of the donkey herd, listening plays a crucial role in maintaining harmony and cohesion. Donkeys communicate with one another through a complex system of vocalizations, body language, and facial expressions, each member of the herd attuned to the needs and emotions of the others. By listening attentively to the cues of their companions, donkeys foster a sense of unity and mutual respect that is essential for their survival and well-being.

3. Cultivating Presence and Awareness: At the heart of listening lies the practice of presence and awareness—the ability to be fully present in the moment and attuned to the subtleties of our surroundings. Donkeys excel in this practice, their senses finely attuned to the sights, sounds, and smells of the world around them. By cultivating a similar sense of presence and awareness in our own lives, we can deepen our connection to ourselves, to others, and to the world at large.

4. Nurturing Empathy and Understanding: Listening is not merely a passive act; it is an active practice that requires empathy and understanding. Donkeys possess an innate ability to empathize with the emotions of others, tuning into the feelings and needs of their companions with remarkable sensitivity. In their empathetic listening, they create a space of safety and trust where others feel seen, heard, and understood.

5. Leading by Example: Ultimately, the donkey's mastery of listening serves as a powerful example for us all—a reminder of the transformative power that lies in the simple act of paying attention. By embodying the virtues of presence, awareness, empathy, and understanding exemplified by the donkey, we can cultivate deeper connections with ourselves, with others, and with the world around us, leading to greater harmony, compassion, and well-being for all.

The power of listening is not confined to the words we hear or the conversations we engage in; rather, it lies in the space between the words, in the silent presence that speaks volumes without saying a word. By embracing the wisdom of the donkey and learning to listen with an open heart and mind, we can tap into a wellspring of insight, understanding, and connection that has the power to transform our lives and the world around us.

- Tuning into the Silent Wisdom of Donkeys

In a world filled with noise and distractions, the silent wisdom of donkeys offers a profound reminder of the importance of tuning into the quieter aspects of life. In this section, we will explore how the simple presence of a donkey can teach us valuable lessons about the power of silence and stillness.

1. Embracing the Language of Silence: Donkeys are masters of communication without words. Through subtle gestures, expressions, and body language, they convey a wealth of information to those who are attuned to their silent language. By observing the quiet interactions between donkeys, we can learn to tune into the subtle nuances of communication that lie beyond the realm of speech.

2. Finding Peace in Stillness: In the presence of a donkey, there is a palpable sense of peace and tranquility—a reminder of the importance of finding moments of stillness amidst the chaos of daily life. By simply being in the company of a donkey, we can experience a sense of calmness and serenity that transcends words and thoughts, grounding us in the present moment and allowing us to find solace in the silence.

3. Cultivating Presence and Awareness: Donkeys possess a keen awareness of their surroundings, attuned to the sights, sounds, and sensations of the world around them. By emulating their sense of presence and awareness, we can learn to become more mindful and attentive to the present moment, fully immersing ourselves in the richness of life as it unfolds.

4. Listening with an Open Heart: In the quiet presence of a donkey, there is an invitation to listen with an open heart—to tune into the wisdom that lies beyond words and to connect with the deeper truths of our own inner being. By quieting the mind and opening ourselves to the silent wisdom of the donkey, we can gain insights and understanding that transcend the limitations of language and logic.

5. Leading by Example: Ultimately, the silent wisdom of donkeys serves as a powerful example for us all—a reminder of the importance of embracing the quieter aspects of life and tuning into the wisdom that lies beyond words. By embodying the virtues of stillness, presence, and attentive listening exemplified by the donkey, we can cultivate a deeper sense of peace, clarity, and connection in our own lives, leading to greater harmony and well-being for ourselves and others.

The silent wisdom of donkeys offers a profound invitation to slow down, quiet the mind, and tune into the deeper rhythms of life. By embracing their gentle presence and attentive listening, we can learn to cultivate a greater sense of peace, presence, and awareness in our own lives, leading to a deeper understanding of ourselves and the world around us.

- **Enhancing Communication through Active Listening**

In a world where communication is often characterized by noise and distraction, the practice of active listening offers a powerful antidote—a way to connect more deeply with others and foster meaningful relationships. In this section, we will explore how the principles of active listening can be applied to enhance communication and cultivate deeper connections with those around us.

1. Being Fully Present: Active listening begins with being fully present in the moment—setting aside distractions and giving our undivided attention to the speaker. By focusing on the speaker's words, tone, and body language, we can tune into the deeper nuances of communication and gain a deeper understanding of their message.

2. Showing Empathy and Understanding: Empathy lies at the heart of active listening—a willingness to step into the shoes of the speaker and see the world from their perspective. By listening with empathy and understanding, we validate the speaker's feelings and experiences, creating a safe and supportive space for them to express themselves openly and honestly.

3. Asking Open-Ended Questions: Active listening involves more than just passively receiving information; it also requires active engagement and participation in the conversation. By asking open-ended questions and seeking clarification when needed, we demonstrate our interest and curiosity in the speaker's thoughts and feelings, encouraging them to delve deeper into their experiences.

4. Reflecting and Paraphrasing: One of the key techniques of active listening is reflecting and paraphrasing the speaker's words back to them in our own words. This not only demonstrates that we are actively listening and understanding their message but also helps to clarify any misunderstandings and ensure that both parties are on the same page.

5. Respecting Silence and Nonverbal Cues: Silence and nonverbal cues play a crucial role in communication, often conveying more meaning than words alone. By respecting moments of silence and paying attention to the speaker's body language and facial expressions, we can gain valuable insights into their thoughts and emotions, deepening our understanding of their message.

Active listening is not merely a skill to be mastered but a way of being—a way of engaging with the world and those around us with openness, empathy, and curiosity. By cultivating the practice of active listening in our own lives, we can enhance our communication skills, foster deeper connections with others, and create a more harmonious and supportive environment for all.

Chapter 5: Finding Joy in the Simple Things

In a world often consumed by the pursuit of material wealth and external validation, the humble donkey offers a poignant reminder of the joy that can be found in the simplest of pleasures. In this chapter, we will explore how the practice of finding joy in the simple things can lead to a deeper sense of fulfillment and contentment in our lives.

1. Cultivating Gratitude: At the heart of finding joy in the simple things lies the practice of gratitude—the ability to appreciate and savor the blessings that surround us each day. Whether it's the warmth of the sun on our face, the laughter of loved ones, or the beauty of a blooming flower, there is no shortage of simple pleasures to be grateful for. By cultivating a spirit of gratitude, we can shift our focus from what we lack to what we have, leading to greater happiness and fulfillment.

2. Embracing Mindfulness: Mindfulness is the practice of being fully present in the moment, paying attention to the sights, sounds, and sensations of our immediate experience. When we approach life with mindfulness, we open ourselves up to the richness of each moment, finding joy in the simple act of being alive. Whether it's savoring a delicious meal, taking a leisurely walk in nature, or spending time with loved ones, mindfulness allows us to fully immerse ourselves in the present moment and find joy in the simple things.

3. Nurturing Connection: Connection is essential to our sense of well-being, and it is often found in the simple moments of human interaction. Whether it's sharing a heartfelt conversation with a friend, giving someone a hug, or lending a helping hand to a stranger, there is joy to be found in the connections we forge with others. By nurturing these connections and cultivating meaningful relationships, we can experience a profound sense of belonging and fulfillment.

4. Seeking Beauty in the Everyday: Beauty surrounds us at every turn, waiting to be discovered in the most unlikely of places. Whether it's the intricate patterns of a snowflake, the vibrant colors of a sunset, or the gentle melody of birdsong, there is beauty to be found in the everyday moments of life. By seeking out and appreciating the beauty that surrounds us, we can find joy in the simplest of things and enrich our lives in profound and meaningful ways.

5. Leading by Example: Ultimately, finding joy in the simple things is not just a personal practice—it's a way of living that can inspire and uplift those around us. By leading by example and embodying the principles of gratitude, mindfulness, connection, and beauty in our own lives, we can inspire others to do the same, creating a ripple effect of joy and positivity that extends far beyond ourselves.

The practice of finding joy in the simple things is a powerful antidote to the complexities and stresses of modern life. By embracing gratitude, mindfulness, connection, and beauty, we can cultivate a deeper sense of fulfillment and contentment, leading to a life that is rich, meaningful, and joyous.

- Donkeys and Delight: Embracing Life's Simple Pleasures

In the presence of a donkey, there is an undeniable sense of delight—a reminder of the joy that can be found in the simplest of pleasures. In this section, we will explore how the companionship of donkeys and the appreciation of life's simple joys can bring a sense of delight and fulfillment to our lives.

1. The Beauty of Connection: Donkeys have a unique ability to forge deep connections with those around them, offering companionship and comfort to all who cross their path. Whether it's the gentle nuzzle of a muzzle or the warmth of their presence by our side, the companionship of donkeys reminds us of the joy that comes from nurturing meaningful connections with others.

2. The Serenity of Nature: Donkeys are creatures of the earth, at home in the natural world and deeply attuned to its rhythms and cycles. Spending time in the company of donkeys allows us to reconnect with the beauty and serenity of nature, finding delight in the simple pleasures of a sunlit meadow, a gentle breeze, or the chorus of birdsong.

3. The Pleasure of Presence: In a world filled with distractions and demands, the quiet presence of a donkey offers a welcome respite—a chance to slow down, be still, and savor the richness of the present moment. Whether it's sitting quietly beside a donkey, feeling the warmth of their fur beneath our fingertips, or simply basking in their serene gaze, the presence of donkeys reminds us of the joy that comes from being fully present in the here and now.

4. The Joy of Simple Pleasures: Donkeys find delight in the simplest of pleasures—a mouthful of fresh grass, a playful romp with friends, or a leisurely stroll in the sunshine. By following their lead and embracing life's simple pleasures, we can cultivate a deeper sense of joy and contentment in our own lives, finding delight in the everyday moments that make life truly worth living.

5. The Gift of Gratitude: Finally, the companionship of donkeys invites us to cultivate an attitude of gratitude—to appreciate and celebrate the blessings that surround us each day. Whether it's the love of family and friends, the beauty of the natural world, or the simple joys of everyday life, the companionship of donkeys reminds us to be grateful for all that we have and to find delight in the abundance of blessings that surround us.

The companionship of donkeys and the appreciation of life's simple pleasures go hand in hand, offering a pathway to greater joy, fulfillment, and contentment in our lives. By embracing the delight that comes from nurturing connections, savoring nature, being present, enjoying simple pleasures, and cultivating gratitude, we can experience a deeper sense of joy and fulfillment, enriching our lives and the lives of those around us in the process.

- Cultivating Joy Amidst Life's Challenges

Life is filled with challenges and uncertainties, but even in the midst of adversity, there are opportunities to cultivate joy and find moments of delight. In this section, we will explore how the steadfast presence of donkeys can inspire us to embrace joy and resilience, even in the face of life's toughest trials.

1. Finding Solace in Connection: Donkeys have an innate ability to offer solace and companionship during difficult times. Their gentle presence and unwavering support serve as a reminder that we are not alone in our struggles. By nurturing connections with loved ones, friends, and even animal companions, we can find comfort and strength in the midst of life's challenges.

2. Seeking Beauty in Unexpected Places: Even in the darkest moments, there is beauty to be found for those who have eyes to see. Donkeys remind us to seek out the beauty and wonder that surrounds us, even in the most unexpected places. By cultivating a sense of wonder and appreciation for the world around us, we can find joy amidst life's challenges and discover moments of grace and beauty in the most unlikely of circumstances.

3. Embracing Resilience and Adaptability: Donkeys are masters of resilience, able to weather the storms of life with grace and dignity. Their ability to adapt to changing circumstances serves as a powerful example for us all, reminding us of the importance of resilience in the face of adversity. By embracing change and learning to adapt to life's challenges, we can cultivate a sense of resilience that allows us to thrive, even in the most difficult of circumstances.

4. Practicing Gratitude and Mindfulness: Gratitude and mindfulness are powerful practices that can help us find joy and contentment, even in the midst of life's challenges. By focusing on the present moment and cultivating an attitude of gratitude for the blessings in our lives, we can shift our perspective and find joy in the midst of difficulty. Donkeys teach us to appreciate the simple pleasures of life, reminding us that even in the midst of struggle, there is much to be grateful for.

5. Choosing Joy as an Act of Resistance: In times of adversity, choosing joy can be an act of resistance—a way of asserting our resilience and refusing to be defined by our circumstances. Donkeys remind us that joy is not contingent on external factors, but rather a choice that we can make each day, regardless of what life may throw our way. By choosing joy in the face of adversity, we reclaim our power and assert our ability to find meaning and purpose, even in the most challenging of times.

The steadfast presence of donkeys serves as a reminder that joy is not dependent on external circumstances, but rather a state of being that we can cultivate from within. By nurturing connections, seeking beauty, embracing resilience, practicing gratitude, and choosing joy, we can find moments of delight and contentment amidst life's challenges, enriching our lives and the lives of those around us in the process.

Chapter 6: Endurance Through Adversity

In the journey of life, adversity is inevitable. Yet, it is in the face of adversity that we often discover our greatest reservoirs of strength and resilience. In this chapter, we will explore how the enduring spirit of donkeys can inspire us to persevere and thrive, even in the most challenging of circumstances.

1. The Steadfast Resolve of Donkeys: Donkeys are renowned for their steadfast resolve and unwavering determination. Whether traversing rocky terrain or carrying heavy burdens, they face adversity with a quiet strength that is both inspiring and humbling. By observing the resilience of donkeys, we can learn valuable lessons about perseverance and endurance in the face of hardship.

2. Navigating Life's Rocky Terrain: Life is often compared to a journey, filled with ups and downs, twists, and turns. Like donkeys navigating rocky terrain, we encounter obstacles and challenges that test our resolve and resilience. By drawing upon the example of donkeys, we can learn to navigate life's rocky terrain with grace and determination, trusting in our ability to overcome adversity and emerge stronger on the other side.

3. Finding Strength in Community: Donkeys are social animals, often found in the company of others. In times of adversity, they rely on the support and camaraderie of their herd to weather the storm. By fostering connections with others and leaning on our community for support, we can find strength and resilience in the face of adversity, knowing that we are not alone in our struggles.

4. Embracing Adaptability and Flexibility: Donkeys are masters of adaptability, able to thrive in a wide range of environments and circumstances. Their ability to adjust to changing conditions serves as a powerful example for us all, reminding us of the importance of flexibility and resilience in the face of adversity. By embracing change and learning to adapt to new challenges, we can cultivate a sense of resilience that allows us to thrive, even in the most difficult of circumstances.

5. Perseverance as a Path to Growth: Ultimately, the enduring spirit of donkeys teaches us that adversity is not merely a test of our strength, but an opportunity for growth and transformation. By embracing adversity as a natural part of the journey of life, we can cultivate resilience, perseverance, and inner strength, leading to greater personal growth and self-discovery in the process.

The enduring spirit of donkeys serves as a powerful reminder of the resilience and strength that lies within each of us. By drawing upon their example and embracing adversity as an opportunity for growth and transformation, we can cultivate the resilience and endurance needed to thrive in the face of life's challenges, emerging stronger, wiser, and more resilient than ever before.

- Tales of Resilience: How Donkeys Persevere

Within the sturdy frame of a donkey lies a heart brimming with resilience, a spirit that refuses to yield in the face of adversity. In this section, we delve into the tales of resilience embodied by these humble creatures, learning from their unwavering perseverance in the face of life's trials.

1. The Journey of Endurance: Picture a rugged mountain path, winding its way through steep cliffs and treacherous terrain. This is the domain of the donkey, where their endurance is put to the ultimate test. Tales abound of donkeys traversing miles of rocky trails, bearing heavy loads with unwavering determination. Their resilience in the face of such challenges serves as a testament to the indomitable spirit that resides within them.

2. The Burden Bearer's Resolve: From dawn until dusk, donkeys toil tirelessly under the weight of burdens—be it sacks of grain, bundles of firewood, or weary travelers. Yet, despite the strain on their backs and the weariness in their limbs, they press onward with a quiet resolve that knows no bounds. Their steadfast determination to fulfill their duties, no matter the cost, inspires awe and admiration in all who witness their perseverance.

3. Surviving Nature's Wrath: Nature can be both friend and foe to the donkey, subjecting them to the whims of the elements—fierce storms, scorching heat, bitter cold. Yet, through it all, they endure, drawing upon their innate resilience to weather the storm. Tales abound of donkeys braving raging rivers, braving blizzards, and seeking shelter from the harsh desert sun, their unwavering resilience a testament to their ability to survive and thrive in even the harshest of conditions.

4. Bonds That Endure: Donkeys are social creatures, forming deep bonds with their companions that withstand the test of time. In times of adversity, they rely on the strength of these bonds to see them through, drawing comfort and support from the companionship of their herd. Tales abound of donkeys standing shoulder to shoulder, facing adversity together with unwavering solidarity—a testament to the resilience that lies within the bonds of friendship and community.

5. Lessons of Resilience: In the tales of resilience embodied by donkeys, we find valuable lessons for navigating our own journey through life's trials. Their unwavering perseverance in the face of adversity teaches us the importance of resilience, determination, and fortitude in overcoming obstacles and achieving our goals. By drawing upon the tales of resilience embodied by donkeys, we can find inspiration and strength to persevere in the face of life's challenges, emerging stronger, wiser, and more resilient than ever before.

The tales of resilience embodied by donkeys serve as a powerful reminder of the strength and fortitude that lie within each of us. By drawing upon their example and embracing the lessons of resilience they offer, we can navigate life's trials with courage and determination, emerging triumphant in the face of adversity.

- Building Resilience in the Face of Obstacles

Life is a journey filled with obstacles and challenges, yet it is through overcoming these trials that we grow and develop resilience. In this section, we will explore how the steadfast nature of donkeys can inspire us to build resilience in the face of adversity.

1. **Embracing Adversity as Growth:** Donkeys encounter obstacles regularly, whether it be navigating difficult terrain or carrying heavy loads. Rather than succumbing to defeat, they face these challenges head-on, viewing them as opportunities for growth and learning. By adopting a similar mindset and embracing adversity as a catalyst for personal development, we can cultivate resilience and thrive in the face of obstacles.

2. **Persistence Amidst Difficulty:** Donkeys are renowned for their persistence, never giving up in the

face of difficulty. They will continue to plod forward, one step at a time, until they reach their destination. By embodying the persistence of donkeys, we can overcome setbacks and persevere in pursuit of our goals, knowing that success often lies just beyond the next hurdle.

3. Seeking Support and Connection: Donkeys are social animals that rely on the support of their herd to navigate life's challenges. They draw strength from their companionship, standing together in solidarity against adversity. Similarly, by seeking support and connection with others, we can bolster our resilience and weather life's storms with greater ease.

4. Adapting to Change: Donkeys are adaptable creatures, able to thrive in a variety of environments and circumstances. They possess a flexibility that allows them to adjust to changing conditions and overcome unexpected obstacles. By cultivating a similar ability to adapt to change, we can navigate life's uncertainties with resilience and grace, embracing new opportunities and overcoming obstacles with ease.

5. Cultivating Self-Compassion: Despite their strength and resilience, donkeys are also gentle creatures that deserve kindness and compassion. In the face of adversity, they do not berate themselves for their perceived shortcomings but instead approach challenges with a sense of self-compassion and acceptance. By treating ourselves with the same kindness and understanding, we can build resilience from within, fostering a sense of inner strength and resilience that carries us through life's trials.

The steadfast nature of donkeys serves as a powerful reminder that resilience is not just about bouncing back from adversity but also about growing stronger in the process. By embracing challenges as opportunities for growth, persisting in the face of difficulty, seeking support and connection, adapting to change, and cultivating self-compassion, we can build resilience and thrive in the face of life's obstacles.

Chapter 7: Navigating Life's Trails with Grace

Life's journey is filled with twists and turns, trials and triumphs. In this chapter, we explore the graceful navigation of life's trails exemplified by the noble donkey, drawing lessons on how to move through life's challenges with poise and dignity.

1. Cultivating Equanimity: Donkeys possess a serene presence, navigating even the most rugged terrain with a sense of calmness and composure. By cultivating equanimity—the ability to remain steady and balanced in the face of adversity—we can navigate life's trails with grace, maintaining our inner peace and perspective amidst the ups and downs of life.

2. Embracing Acceptance: Donkeys are masters of acceptance, embracing each moment as it comes without resistance or judgment. Their willingness to accept life on its own terms allows them to move through challenges with grace and ease. By adopting a similar attitude of acceptance, we can release the burden of resistance and flow more effortlessly with the currents of life.

3. Finding Balance: Balanced and sure-footed, donkeys traverse uneven terrain with grace and precision. They embody the importance of finding balance in all aspects of life—physical, mental, and emotional. By prioritizing self-care, setting healthy boundaries, and nurturing our well-being, we can cultivate the inner balance needed to navigate life's trails with grace and resilience.

4. Trusting Intuition: Donkeys possess a keen sense of intuition, trusting their instincts to guide them safely through unfamiliar territory. By honing our own intuition and learning to trust the wisdom of our inner voice, we can navigate life's trails with confidence and clarity, knowing that we are always guided by our inner compass.

5. Practicing Patience: Patience is a virtue embodied by the noble donkey, which moves at its own pace, never rushing or hurrying. By practicing patience—both with ourselves and with others—we can navigate life's trails with grace and humility, allowing things to unfold in their own time and trusting in the wisdom of the journey.

Navigating life's trails with grace is not about avoiding obstacles or challenges, but rather about embracing them as opportunities for growth and learning. By cultivating equanimity, embracing acceptance, finding balance, trusting intuition, and practicing patience, we can move through life's trails with grace and dignity, emerging stronger and more resilient with each step of the journey.

- Grace Under Pressure: Lessons in Gracefulness from Donkeys

In the hustle and bustle of life, the gentle demeanor of donkeys offers a profound lesson in maintaining grace under pressure. In this section, we explore the qualities that embody gracefulness as exemplified by these noble creatures, drawing inspiration from their serene presence and steadfast resilience.

1. Serenity Amidst Chaos: In the midst of chaos and commotion, donkeys exude a sense of calmness and serenity that is truly remarkable. Their unruffled demeanor serves as a reminder that gracefulness is not about avoiding challenges, but about maintaining inner peace and composure amidst life's storms.

2. Poise in Motion: Whether navigating rocky terrain or carrying heavy burdens, donkeys move with a grace and poise that is both elegant and effortless. Their sure-footedness and steady gait serve as a testament to the power of gracefulness in action, inspiring us to move through life's challenges with confidence and grace.

3. Patience as a Virtue: Donkeys are renowned for their patience, able to endure long hours of labor without complaint. Their quiet perseverance in the face of adversity serves as a powerful example of gracefulness under pressure, reminding us of the importance of patience and resilience in navigating life's trials.

4. Acceptance of What Is: Donkeys possess a remarkable ability to accept life on its own terms, embracing each moment with equanimity and grace. Their willingness to surrender to the flow of life serves as a lesson in letting go of resistance and finding peace amidst uncertainty.

5. Strength in Gentleness: Despite their size and strength, donkeys are gentle creatures at heart, showing kindness and compassion to those around them. Their ability to exhibit strength without aggression serves as a powerful example of gracefulness in interpersonal relationships, inspiring us to cultivate empathy and understanding in our interactions with others.

The lessons in gracefulness from donkeys remind us that true strength lies not in forcefulness or aggression, but in serenity, poise, patience, acceptance, and gentleness. By embodying these qualities in our own lives, we can navigate life's challenges with grace and dignity, inspiring others to do the same and creating a more harmonious and compassionate world in the process.

- Maintaining Gracefulness Through Life's Twists and Turns

Life is a journey filled with unexpected twists and turns, yet it is in these moments of uncertainty that gracefulness shines the brightest. In this section, we explore how the steadfast nature of donkeys can inspire us to maintain gracefulness as we navigate the ever-changing landscape of life.

1. Embracing Flexibility: Donkeys are masters of adaptation, able to navigate diverse terrains with ease and grace. Their flexibility in the face of change serves as a reminder that rigidity only breeds resistance, while flexibility allows us to flow with the natural rhythms of life.

2. Responding with Resilience: Life's twists and turns often present us with unforeseen challenges and obstacles. Like the donkey, we can respond to these challenges with resilience, drawing upon our inner strength and resourcefulness to overcome adversity and emerge stronger on the other side.

3. Cultivating Equanimity: Maintaining gracefulness in the midst of life's ups and downs requires a sense of equanimity—a steady and balanced approach to both joy and sorrow. By cultivating equanimity, we can remain grounded and centered, regardless of the circumstances swirling around us.

4. Practicing Presence: Donkeys live in the present moment, fully engaged with the here and now. Similarly, by practicing presence and mindfulness, we can navigate life's twists and turns with greater clarity and awareness, making conscious choices that align with our values and aspirations.

5. Trusting in the Journey: Just as a donkey trusts its rider to guide it safely through unknown terrain, we can trust in the journey of life, knowing that each twist and turn holds valuable lessons and opportunities for growth. By embracing the journey with an open heart and mind, we can maintain gracefulness even in the face of uncertainty.

Maintaining gracefulness through life's twists and turns is not about avoiding challenges or hardships, but about embracing them as integral parts of the journey. By embodying the qualities of flexibility, resilience, equanimity, presence, and trust, we can navigate life's ever-changing landscape with poise, dignity, and grace, inspiring others to do the same along the way.

Chapter 8: Loyalty and Trust

In a world where relationships are often fleeting and trust is hard to come by, the unwavering loyalty and trustworthiness of donkeys stand as a shining example of steadfast companionship. In this chapter, we explore the profound lessons of loyalty and trust that we can learn from these noble creatures.

1. The Bond of Trust: At the heart of every relationship lies a foundation of trust, built upon mutual respect and reliability. Donkeys exemplify the essence of trustworthiness, forming deep bonds with those who earn their trust through consistent kindness and care. By honoring our commitments and demonstrating integrity in our actions, we can cultivate trust in our relationships, fostering deeper connections and lasting bonds.

2. Loyalty Beyond Measure: Donkeys are fiercely loyal creatures, standing by their companions through thick and thin. Whether serving as a pack animal, a guardian of the herd, or a beloved companion, they remain steadfast in their loyalty, never wavering in their commitment to those they hold dear. By cultivating loyalty in our own lives—standing by our loved ones through adversity and remaining true to our values and convictions—we can nurture relationships that withstand the test of time.

3. Building Bridges of Understanding: Trust and loyalty are not only about actions but also about empathy and understanding. Donkeys possess a remarkable ability to empathize with the emotions of those around them, forging bonds of trust and loyalty through their compassionate presence. By seeking to understand the perspectives and experiences of others, we can bridge divides, build trust, and foster deeper connections in our relationships.

4. Honoring Boundaries and Respect: Respect is an essential component of trust and loyalty, requiring us to honor the boundaries and autonomy of those around us. Donkeys demonstrate a profound respect for the space and needs of their companions, fostering an environment of mutual respect and cooperation. By respecting the boundaries and autonomy of others, we can create relationships built on trust, loyalty, and mutual understanding.

5. Forgiveness and Grace: Even in moments of misunderstanding or conflict, donkeys offer lessons in forgiveness and grace. Their capacity for forgiveness allows them to move past transgressions and strengthen the bonds of trust and loyalty that bind them to their companions. By extending forgiveness and grace to others—and to ourselves—we can heal rifts, restore trust, and deepen our connections with those we hold dear.

The lessons of loyalty and trust embodied by donkeys remind us of the importance of cultivating strong and enduring relationships built on mutual respect, understanding, and compassion. By honoring our commitments, demonstrating loyalty, fostering understanding, respecting boundaries, and extending forgiveness, we can nurture relationships that stand the test of time, bringing richness and meaning to our lives in the process.

- Loyalty Unbridled: The Donkey's Unwavering Commitment

In a world where loyalty can often be fleeting, the steadfast devotion of donkeys stands as a beacon of unwavering commitment. In this section, we delve into the profound depths of loyalty demonstrated by these noble creatures, drawing inspiration from their unwavering dedication to those they hold dear.

1. Guardians of Trust: Donkeys are renowned for their unwavering commitment to those they trust, serving as guardians of trust and reliability in the lives of their companions. Whether carrying burdens, standing watch over the herd, or offering comfort in times of need, they remain steadfast in their loyalty, earning the trust and admiration of all who encounter them.

2. Companions Through Thick and Thin: Through life's trials and tribulations, donkeys stand by their companions with unwavering loyalty and support. Their steadfast presence serves as a source of comfort and reassurance, reminding us that we are never alone in our journey. By cultivating relationships built on mutual trust and loyalty, we can weather life's storms with greater resilience and fortitude.

3. Trust Earned, Not Given: Donkeys do not offer their loyalty lightly; it must be earned through consistent kindness, care, and respect. Once earned, however, their loyalty knows no bounds, enduring through the passage of time and the trials of life. By demonstrating integrity, reliability, and compassion in our interactions with others, we can earn their trust and loyalty, forging bonds that stand the test of time.

4. Loyalty Beyond Words: Donkeys may not express their loyalty in words, but their actions speak volumes. From the gentle nuzzle of their muzzle to the steadfastness of their gaze, they communicate their unwavering commitment through gestures of kindness, devotion, and companionship. By observing the subtle cues of loyalty demonstrated by donkeys, we can learn to deepen our connections with others and nurture relationships built on trust and mutual respect.

5. The Gift of Loyalty: In a world where loyalty is often undervalued, the gift of loyalty bestowed by donkeys is truly precious. Their unwavering commitment serves as a reminder of the power of loyalty to enrich our lives and strengthen our bonds with those we hold dear. By cherishing and reciprocating the loyalty of others, we can create a world filled with trust, compassion, and unwavering support.

The loyalty demonstrated by donkeys serves as a powerful reminder of the profound impact that unwavering commitment can have on our lives. By honoring the trust placed in us, demonstrating loyalty to those we hold dear, and fostering relationships built on mutual respect and understanding, we can cultivate a world where loyalty reins supreme, enriching our lives and the lives of those around us in countless ways.

- **Nurturing Trust and Loyalty in Human Relationships**

In a world where genuine connections are treasured, nurturing trust and loyalty in human relationships is paramount for fostering deep and meaningful connections. Drawing inspiration from the unwavering commitment of donkeys, let's explore how we can cultivate trust and loyalty in our interactions with others.

1. Consistency and Reliability: Like donkeys, we can nurture trust and loyalty by demonstrating consistency and reliability in our actions. By following through on our promises, showing up for others when they need us, and being dependable in times of both joy and adversity, we lay the foundation for strong and enduring relationships.

2. Open Communication and Transparency: Effective communication is essential for building trust and loyalty in relationships. Just as donkeys rely on subtle cues to communicate with their companions, we can foster trust by being open, honest, and transparent in our interactions. By expressing our thoughts and feelings openly and listening with empathy and understanding, we create an environment where trust can flourish.

3. Respect for Boundaries and Autonomy: Respecting the boundaries and autonomy of others is essential for nurturing trust and loyalty in relationships. Just as donkeys honor the personal space of their companions, we can show respect by recognizing and honoring the boundaries of others. By allowing individuals the freedom to express themselves authentically and make their own choices, we cultivate trust and loyalty based on mutual respect and understanding.

4. Empathy and Compassion: Empathy and compassion are fundamental for fostering trust and loyalty in human relationships. Like donkeys, who offer comfort and support to their companions in times of need, we can nurture trust by showing empathy and compassion towards others. By acknowledging and validating their emotions, offering a listening ear, and providing support without judgment, we deepen our connections and strengthen the bonds of loyalty.

5. Forgiveness and Grace: Inevitably, conflicts and misunderstandings will arise in any relationship. Just as donkeys exemplify forgiveness and grace, we can nurture trust and loyalty by extending forgiveness and grace to others. By letting go of resentments, offering second chances, and approaching conflicts with empathy and understanding, we create space for healing and growth, strengthening our relationships in the process.

Nurturing trust and loyalty in human relationships requires intention, effort, and commitment. By embodying the qualities of consistency, open communication, respect, empathy, and forgiveness, we can cultivate deep and meaningful connections that stand the test of time, enriching our lives and the lives of those around us immeasurably.

Chapter 9: The Art of Self-Preservation

In the journey of life, self-preservation is an essential skill that allows us to navigate challenges, protect our well-being, and thrive amidst adversity. Drawing inspiration from the instinctual wisdom of donkeys, this chapter explores the art of self-preservation and its importance in achieving balance and resilience.

1. Instinctual Survival Tactics: Donkeys possess innate survival instincts honed by centuries of evolution. From sensing danger to finding shelter, they demonstrate the art of self-preservation through their ability to navigate their environment with caution and awareness. By tuning into our own instincts and intuition, we can cultivate a deeper connection with ourselves and make choices that prioritize our safety and well-being.

2. Setting Boundaries: Boundaries serve as a vital component of self-preservation, helping us define our limits and protect our physical, emotional, and mental health. Like donkeys that establish their territory and defend it against intruders, we can assert boundaries that safeguard our personal space, time, and energy, allowing us to maintain a sense of balance and autonomy in our lives.

3. Prioritizing Self-Care: Self-care is an essential aspect of self-preservation, encompassing practices that nourish and replenish our body, mind, and spirit. Just as donkeys seek out rest and nourishment to replenish their energy reserves, we can prioritize self-care by engaging in activities that promote relaxation, rejuvenation, and overall well-being, ensuring that we have the resilience to face life's challenges with strength and vitality.

4. Cultivating Resilience: Resilience is the ability to bounce back from adversity and thrive in the face of challenges. Donkeys exemplify resilience through their ability to endure hardships and adapt to changing circumstances. By cultivating resilience in our own lives—building coping skills, fostering optimism, and embracing challenges as opportunities for growth—we can navigate life's ups and downs with greater ease and grace, strengthening our capacity for self-preservation in the process.

5. Seeking Support: Just as donkeys seek safety in the company of their herd, we can cultivate self-preservation by seeking support from trusted friends, family, or professionals when needed. By reaching out for help, sharing our struggles, and leaning on others for support, we can lighten our burdens and find strength in community, bolstering our resilience and enhancing our ability to preserve our well-being amidst life's challenges.

The art of self-preservation is a multifaceted endeavor that encompasses tuning into our instincts, setting boundaries, prioritizing self-care, cultivating resilience, and seeking support when needed. By drawing inspiration from the wisdom of donkeys and embracing these principles in our own lives, we can navigate the journey of life with greater ease, balance, and resilience, preserving our well-being and flourishing amidst adversity.

- Survival Instincts: Donkeys and the Art of Self-Preservation

In the wild and in the domesticated world alike, donkeys exhibit remarkable survival instincts that serve as a blueprint for mastering the art of self-preservation. In this segment, we delve into the innate wisdom of donkeys and their ability to navigate life's challenges with grace and resilience.

1. Heightened Awareness: Donkeys possess a keen sense of awareness, attuned to the subtlest changes in their surroundings. From detecting potential threats to sensing changes in weather patterns, their heightened awareness allows them to anticipate danger and take proactive measures to ensure their safety. By cultivating mindfulness and staying present in the moment, we can sharpen our own senses and enhance our ability to respond effectively to the challenges that arise in our lives.

2. Adaptive Behaviors: Adaptability is a hallmark of survival, and donkeys excel in adapting to diverse environments and changing circumstances. Whether foraging for food in arid landscapes or seeking shelter during inclement weather, they demonstrate a remarkable ability to adapt their behaviors to meet their basic needs. By embracing flexibility and learning to adapt to changing conditions, we can enhance our resilience and increase our chances of thriving in even the most challenging of environments.

3. Vigilance and Caution: Donkeys are naturally cautious animals, exercising vigilance to assess potential threats and risks in their environment. Their cautious demeanor serves as a protective mechanism, allowing them to avoid dangerous situations and minimize their exposure to harm. By adopting a similar approach of vigilance and caution in our own lives, we can mitigate risks and safeguard our well-being, ensuring that we are better equipped to navigate the uncertainties of the world around us.

4. Preservation of Energy: Energy conservation is essential for survival, and donkeys excel in preserving their energy reserves for times of need. Whether resting in the shade during the heat of the day or conserving energy during periods of scarcity, they prioritize the preservation of their physical resources as a means of ensuring their survival. By practicing moderation, pacing ourselves, and avoiding unnecessary exertion, we can conserve our own energy and maintain our vitality in the face of life's demands.

5. Social Cohesion: Donkeys are social animals, often forming close-knit bonds with members of their herd as a means of enhancing their collective security and well-being. Through mutual grooming, vocal communication, and cooperative behaviors, they foster a sense of social cohesion that strengthens their resilience and enhances their chances of survival. By cultivating supportive relationships and fostering a sense of community, we can draw upon the strength of our social networks to navigate life's challenges with greater confidence and resilience.

The survival instincts of donkeys offer valuable insights into the art of self-preservation, highlighting the importance of heightened awareness, adaptive behaviors, vigilance, energy conservation, and social cohesion in ensuring our well-being and resilience in an ever-changing world. By drawing inspiration from the wisdom of donkeys, we can cultivate the skills and strategies needed to thrive amidst life's challenges and emerge stronger and more resilient in the process.

- Balancing Self-Care and Care for Others

In the intricate dance of life, finding harmony between caring for oneself and extending care to others is essential for overall well-being. Drawing inspiration from the balanced nature of donkeys, this segment explores the delicate art of striking a harmonious balance between self-care and care-giving.

1. Nurturing Self-Care: Just as donkeys prioritize their own needs for sustenance and rest, self-care forms the foundation of overall well-being. It involves attending to our physical, emotional, and mental health through practices such as adequate sleep, healthy nutrition, regular exercise, and stress management. By prioritizing self-care, we replenish our energy reserves and cultivate resilience, enabling us to better care for others from a place of strength and vitality.

2. Compassionate Care for Others: Donkeys exhibit a gentle and nurturing demeanor towards their companions, offering support and companionship when needed. Similarly, extending care to others involves showing compassion, empathy, and kindness towards their needs and struggles. Whether lending a listening ear, offering a helping hand, or providing emotional support, compassionate caregiving nurtures connection and fosters a sense of community and belonging.

3. Setting Boundaries: Maintaining balance between self-care and caregiving requires setting healthy boundaries that honor our own needs and limitations. Like donkeys who assert boundaries to protect their personal space and well-being, we too must establish boundaries that safeguard our physical, emotional, and mental health. By recognizing and respecting our own boundaries, we prevent burnout and exhaustion, ensuring that we can continue to care for others effectively over the long term.

4. Cultivating Reciprocity: Healthy relationships are built on a foundation of reciprocity, where care is exchanged mutually between individuals. Donkeys demonstrate reciprocity within their herds, offering support and protection to one another in times of need. Similarly, cultivating reciprocity in our relationships involves both giving and receiving care in a balanced and equitable manner. By fostering a culture of mutual support and generosity, we create environments where everyone's needs are valued and respected.

5. Embracing Flexibility: Balancing self-care and care for others requires flexibility and adaptability to shifting circumstances and priorities. Like donkeys who adjust their behaviors to meet the demands of their environment, we too must be willing to adapt our caregiving practices to accommodate our own evolving needs and those of others. By embracing flexibility, we can navigate the complexities of caregiving with grace and resilience, ensuring that both our own well-being and that of others are prioritized and nurtured.

Finding balance between self-care and care for others is a dynamic and ongoing process that requires intention, compassion, and mindfulness. By drawing inspiration from the balanced nature of donkeys and embracing practices that honor our own needs while also extending care to others, we can create a life rich in harmony, connection, and well-being for ourselves and those around us.

Chapter 10: Respect for Boundaries

Respecting boundaries is a fundamental aspect of healthy relationships, enabling individuals to establish autonomy, safety, and mutual respect. In this chapter, inspired by the innate wisdom of donkeys, we explore the importance of respecting boundaries and fostering harmonious connections.

1. Understanding Personal Boundaries: Boundaries delineate where one person ends and another begins, encompassing physical, emotional, and psychological space. Like donkeys who assert their personal space within the herd, understanding and respecting personal boundaries is essential for cultivating self-awareness, autonomy, and well-being.

2. Communicating Boundaries Effectively: Clear and assertive communication is a key to establishing and maintaining boundaries in relationships. Donkeys communicate boundaries through subtle cues and body language, signaling their comfort levels and preferences to others. Similarly, effective communication empowers individuals to express their needs, limits, and boundaries openly and respectfully.

3. Honoring Consent and Choice: Respecting boundaries entails honoring the principle of consent and choice in all interactions. Just as donkeys respect each other's autonomy within the herd, honoring consent involves seeking permission before engaging in physical contact or sharing personal information. By prioritizing consent and choice, individuals cultivate trust, safety, and mutual respect in their relationships.

4. Boundaries in Conflict Resolution: Boundaries play a crucial role in conflict resolution, providing a framework for navigating disagreements respectfully and constructively. Like donkeys who maintain distance during conflicts to avoid escalation, establishing boundaries allows individuals to assert their needs and preferences while fostering empathy and understanding in resolving conflicts.

5. Cultivating Empathy and Understanding: Empathy and understanding are essential for respecting boundaries and fostering healthy relationships. Just as donkeys demonstrate empathy towards the needs of their companions, cultivating empathy involves recognizing and validating the experiences and boundaries of others. By fostering empathy and understanding, individuals build stronger connections based on mutual respect and compassion.

Respecting boundaries is a cornerstone of fostering healthy, fulfilling relationships built on trust, respect, and mutual understanding. Inspired by the wisdom of donkeys, embracing practices that honor personal autonomy, effective communication, consent, and empathy fosters harmonious connections that enrich the lives of individuals and communities alike.

- Honoring Space: Understanding Donkey Boundaries

Donkeys, like all creatures, have an innate need for personal space and boundaries. In this exploration inspired by the wisdom of these noble animals, we delve into the importance of honoring and understanding the boundaries of donkeys.

1. Physical Boundaries: Donkeys have a clear sense of physical boundaries, respecting their own space and that of others within their herd. Understanding their need for personal space teaches us the importance of respecting physical boundaries in our interactions with them and with each other. Just as donkeys maintain a comfortable distance between themselves and others, we too can learn to respect the physical boundaries of those around us, ensuring a sense of safety and comfort in our relationships.

2. Emotional Boundaries: Emotional boundaries are equally important for donkeys as they navigate their social interactions. They express their feelings and preferences through subtle cues and body language, signaling their need for space or connection. By observing and respecting these emotional boundaries, we can learn valuable lessons in empathy and understanding. Applying these insights to our own interactions, we can communicate our emotions effectively and honor the emotional boundaries of others, fostering deeper connections and mutual respect.

3. Social Dynamics: Within the herd, donkeys establish hierarchies and social structures that dictate their interactions and relationships. They navigate these dynamics with a delicate balance of assertiveness and respect, honoring the boundaries of their companions while asserting their own needs when necessary. By studying these social dynamics, we gain insights into the importance of mutual respect and cooperation in maintaining harmonious relationships. Embracing these principles, we can cultivate healthier social dynamics in our own communities, where boundaries are honored and relationships are built on a foundation of trust and understanding.

4. Communication: Communication is a key to understanding and respecting donkey boundaries. They communicate their needs, boundaries, and emotions through a complex language of vocalizations, body language, and gestures. By learning to interpret these cues, we can better understand their boundaries and respond accordingly. Applying this principle to human interactions, we can enhance our communication skills, express our boundaries clearly and assertively, and listen attentively to the boundaries of others, fostering deeper connections and mutual respect.

5. Mutual Respect: At the heart of it all, honoring donkey boundaries teaches us the importance of mutual respect in all relationships. Whether with animals or fellow humans, respecting boundaries is essential for fostering trust, safety, and harmony. By embracing the principles of mutual respect, we create environments where individuals feel valued, heard, and understood, nurturing healthy relationships built on a foundation of empathy and respect.

Understanding and honoring donkey boundaries offers valuable lessons in empathy, communication, and mutual respect that can enrich our relationships and communities. By applying these insights to our interactions, we can cultivate deeper connections, foster trust and understanding, and create a more compassionate and harmonious world for all beings.

- Establishing Healthy Boundaries for Personal Well-being

In the journey of self-discovery and growth, establishing healthy boundaries is vital for safeguarding our physical, emotional, and mental well-being. Inspired by the wisdom of donkeys, let's explore the importance of setting boundaries and cultivating self-care practices that honor our needs and promote holistic wellness.

1. Identifying Personal Needs: Like donkeys, we must first identify our own needs and priorities to establish effective boundaries. Reflecting on our physical, emotional, and mental well-being allows us to pinpoint areas where boundaries are necessary for self-preservation and balance. By acknowledging our needs without judgment, we empower ourselves to prioritize self-care and set boundaries that support our overall health and happiness.

2. Communicating Boundaries Clearly: Effective communication is essential for articulating boundaries to others in our lives. Just as donkeys convey their boundaries through body language and vocalizations, we can express our limits and preferences assertively and respectfully. Clearly communicating our boundaries ensures that others understand and respect our needs, fostering healthier relationships based on mutual understanding and respect.

3. Prioritizing Self-Care: Setting boundaries is an act of self-care that prioritizes our well-being and nurtures a healthy sense of self-worth. Like donkeys that prioritize rest, nourishment, and relaxation to maintain their vitality, we can prioritize activities that replenish our energy reserves and promote holistic wellness. Engaging in self-care practices such as mindfulness, exercise, creative expression, and relaxation techniques empowers us to nurture our physical, emotional, and mental health.

4. Honoring Limits and Boundaries: Respecting our own limits and boundaries is essential for preventing burnout and maintaining balance in our lives. Donkeys demonstrate the importance of honoring personal space and autonomy within their herds, setting boundaries that protect their well-being. Similarly, we can honor our own boundaries by saying no to activities or commitments that compromise our health or values, and by establishing healthy routines that support our overall well-being.

5. Seeking Support When Needed: As social creatures, seeking support from trusted friends, family, or professionals is essential for maintaining healthy boundaries and promoting well-being. Just as donkeys seek comfort and companionship from their herd members, reaching out for support allows us to navigate challenges and setbacks with resilience and grace. Whether seeking guidance, validation, or encouragement, reaching out for support reinforces our commitment to self-care and fosters a sense of connection and belonging.

Establishing healthy boundaries is an act of self-love and empowerment that honors our inherent worth and promotes holistic well-being. By drawing inspiration from the wisdom of donkeys and prioritizing self-care, effective communication, and self-advocacy, we can create a life that is aligned with our values, needs, and aspirations, fostering a deep sense of fulfillment and joy.

Chapter 11: The Language of Body and Soul

In the intricate tapestry of existence, the language of body and soul intertwines to convey the deepest truths of our being. Drawing inspiration from the profound connection between donkeys' physical presence and inner wisdom, this chapter explores the intricate dialogue between body and soul and its profound implications for self-awareness and spiritual growth.

1. Embodied Wisdom: Donkeys embody a profound wisdom that emanates from their very being, transcending mere physical form. Their presence speaks volumes, conveying a depth of understanding and insight that transcends words. By attuning ourselves to the language of the body, we can access a wellspring of intuitive wisdom that guides us on our journey of self-discovery and personal growth.

2. Listening to the Body's Signals: The body serves as a vessel for the expression of our innermost truths and desires. Like donkeys who communicate through subtle cues and gestures, our bodies speak to us through sensations, emotions, and physical symptoms. By listening attentively to the language of the body, we can uncover hidden messages and insights that illuminate our path and facilitate healing and transformation.

3. Integrating Mind, Body, and Spirit: True harmony arises when mind, body, and spirit are in alignment, working in concert to create a sense of wholeness and vitality. Donkeys exemplify this harmony, embodying a unity of being that transcends dualistic distinctions. By cultivating awareness of the interconnectedness of mind, body, and spirit, we can foster a deeper sense of integration and balance, nurturing our overall well-being and spiritual growth.

4. Sacred Movement and Stillness: Movement and stillness are sacred expressions of the body and soul, offering pathways to deeper self-awareness and connection with the divine. Like donkeys that move with grace and purpose, our bodies have the capacity to express our innermost essence through movement and gesture. Similarly, stillness invites us to journey inward, accessing the depths of our soul and communing with the divine presence within.

5. Embodied Presence in the World: Ultimately, embodying the language of body and soul invites us to inhabit our lives with greater presence and authenticity. By aligning our actions with our inner truth and values, we can live with integrity and purpose, contributing to the greater good with each step we take. Like donkeys that embody a quiet dignity and strength, our presence in the world becomes a beacon of light and inspiration, illuminating the path for ourselves and others on the journey of self-discovery and spiritual awakening.

The language of body and soul speaks to the deepest truths of our existence, inviting us to listen with an open heart and mind. By attuning ourselves to this sacred dialogue, we can access a wellspring of wisdom and insight that guides us on the path to wholeness, healing, and spiritual fulfillment.

- Unspoken Communication: Deciphering Donkey Body Language

In the silent exchange between humans and donkeys lies a rich tapestry of unspoken communication, where subtle gestures and movements convey a wealth of meaning. This exploration delves into the nuanced language of donkey body language, offering insights into their inner world and fostering deeper connections between species.

1. Ears: The ears are perhaps the most expressive feature of a donkey's body, serving as windows to their emotions and intentions. When relaxed and facing forward, they signal contentment and curiosity. Pinned back against the head may indicate discomfort, irritation, or aggression. By observing the position and movement of their ears, we can gain valuable insights into a donkey's state of mind and emotional well-being.

2. Eyes: The eyes of a donkey are mirrors of their soul, reflecting emotions and inner thoughts with clarity and depth. Soft, half-closed eyes convey relaxation and trust, while wide-open eyes may signal alertness or fear. By meeting a donkey's gaze with gentleness and respect, we can establish a connection based on mutual trust and understanding, fostering a sense of safety and security in their presence.

3. Body Posture: The posture of a donkey communicates volumes about their mood and intentions. A relaxed, upright posture indicates confidence and ease, while a hunched or tense stance may suggest discomfort or anxiety. By observing the subtleties of their body language, we can gauge their level of comfort and respond accordingly, creating an environment that promotes their well-being and trust.

4. Vocalizations: Donkeys may vocalize in a variety of ways to express their needs, emotions, and desires. From gentle braying to soft nickers, each vocalization carries its own message and meaning. By attuning ourselves to the nuances of their vocalizations, we can better understand their communication style and respond with empathy and sensitivity to their needs.

5. Tail Movement: The movement of a donkey's tail can offer insights into their emotional state and level of arousal. A relaxed, swaying tail signifies contentment, while rapid or agitated movements may indicate discomfort or excitement. By observing the rhythm and intensity of their tail movements, we can tune into their emotional landscape and respond with care and consideration to their needs.

Deciphering donkey body language is an art that requires patience, observation, and empathy. By attuning ourselves to the subtle cues and signals they offer, we can deepen our understanding of their inner world and cultivate relationships based on mutual trust, respect, and compassion, bridging the divide between species and fostering profound connections that transcend language.

- **Deepening Connections Through Nonverbal Communication**

In the intricate dance of communication, words often pale in comparison to the depth and richness of nonverbal cues. Drawing inspiration from the profound connection between humans and donkeys, this exploration delves into the transformative power of nonverbal communication in deepening connections and fostering meaningful relationships.

1. Presence and Attunement: Nonverbal communication begins with presence—a willingness to be fully engaged and attuned to the other's presence. Like donkeys that possess an innate ability to sense the emotions and intentions of those around them, cultivating presence allows us to tune into the subtle cues and energies that flow between individuals. By being fully present in our interactions, we create a space for genuine connection and mutual understanding to flourish.

2. Body Language and Gestures: Body language and gestures convey a wealth of information about our thoughts, feelings, and intentions. From a warm smile to a reassuring touch, each gesture communicates volumes about our emotional state and level of engagement. Like donkeys that rely on subtle cues such as ear position and tail movement to convey their needs and desires, we can harness the power of body language to express empathy, compassion, and connection, deepening our relationships with others in profound ways.

3. Empathetic Listening: True communication goes beyond words—it involves empathetic listening, where we strive to understand not only the content of the message but also the underlying emotions and needs. Like donkeys who listen with quiet attentiveness to the cues and vocalizations of their companions, empathetic listening requires us to be fully present and attuned to the nuances of nonverbal communication. By listening with empathy and compassion, we create a safe and supportive space for others to express themselves authentically and deepen their sense of connection and belonging.

4. Trust and Vulnerability: Nonverbal communication plays a crucial role in building trust and fostering vulnerability in relationships. Like donkeys that demonstrate trust through gentle gestures and open body language, we can cultivate trust by honoring the nonverbal cues and boundaries of others. By creating a safe and supportive environment where individuals feel seen, heard, and valued, we encourage them to open up and share their thoughts, feelings, and experiences authentically, deepening the bonds of connection and intimacy.

5. Shared Presence in Nature: Nature serves as a powerful backdrop for nonverbal communication, offering a sanctuary where humans and animals alike can connect on a deeper level. Like donkeys that thrive in natural environments, we can deepen our connections through shared experiences in nature—whether it's a peaceful walk in the woods, a quiet moment by the ocean, or a gentle encounter with wildlife. In the embrace of nature's beauty and serenity, nonverbal communication flows effortlessly, transcending language barriers and fostering a sense of unity and interconnectedness with all beings.

Nonverbal communication is a universal language that speaks to the heart and soul of human experience. By embracing presence, empathy, and authenticity in our interactions, we can harness the transformative power of nonverbal cues to deepen connections, cultivate compassion, and foster a more harmonious and interconnected world for all beings.

Chapter 12: Leading with Gentle Guidance

In the realm of leadership, the gentle guidance exemplified by donkeys offers profound insights into fostering trust, cooperation, and growth. This chapter explores the art of leading with gentle guidance, drawing inspiration from the wisdom of donkeys and their natural inclination towards compassionate leadership.

1. Cultivating Presence: At the heart of gentle guidance lies a deep sense of presence—a willingness to be fully engaged and attuned to the needs and emotions of those we lead. Like donkeys who lead with quiet confidence and presence, cultivating presence allows us to create a space for open communication, mutual respect, and collaboration to flourish.

2. Empowering Others: Gentle guidance involves empowering others to discover their own strengths, capabilities, and potential. Rather than imposing authority or control, it is about fostering autonomy and self-reliance in those we lead. Like donkeys that encourage independence and initiative within their herd, empowering others cultivates a sense of ownership and accountability, driving innovation, and fostering growth and development.

3. Leading by Example: Leading with gentle guidance requires leading by example—modeling the values, behaviors, and attitudes we wish to see in others. Like donkeys who exemplify patience, compassion, and resilience in their interactions, leading by example inspires trust, admiration, and loyalty in those we lead. By embodying the qualities of integrity, authenticity, and humility, we create a culture of excellence and excellence that motivates and inspires others to do the same.

4. Nurturing Trust and Collaboration: Trust and collaboration are foundational to effective leadership. Like donkeys that foster cooperation and harmony within their herd through gentle leadership, nurturing trust and collaboration involves building authentic relationships based on mutual respect, transparency, and empathy. By creating a supportive and inclusive environment where everyone's voice is valued and heard, we harness the collective wisdom and creativity of the group, driving innovation, and achieving shared goals.

5. Embracing Adaptability: Effective leadership requires adaptability and flexibility in response to changing circumstances and dynamics. Like donkeys who adapt their leadership style to suit the needs of the group, embracing adaptability allows us to navigate uncertainty and complexity with grace and resilience. By remaining open-minded and receptive to feedback, we continuously evolve and grow as leaders, inspiring confidence and trust in those we lead.

Leading with gentle guidance is about fostering a culture of trust, empowerment, and collaboration that unleashes the full potential of individuals and teams. By drawing inspiration from the wisdom of donkeys and embracing principles of presence, empowerment, leading by example, trust, and adaptability, we can cultivate compassionate leadership that inspires and transforms lives, organizations, and communities for the better.

- Leading with Love: Donkeys as Gentle Leaders

In the realm of leadership, the gentle guidance exhibited by donkeys offers profound lessons in leading with love, compassion, and empathy. This exploration delves into the qualities of donkeys as gentle leaders and the transformative power of love in fostering trust, cooperation, and growth.

1. Compassionate Presence: At the core of donkey leadership lies a compassionate presence—a deep sense of connection and empathy with those they lead. Like donkeys who lead with quiet confidence and empathy, leading with love involves cultivating a presence that fosters trust, openness, and mutual respect among team members.

2. Nurturing Relationships: Donkeys excel in nurturing relationships within their herd, fostering a sense of belonging and camaraderie among members. Leading with love entails building authentic connections and fostering a supportive environment where individuals feel valued, heard, and supported in their growth and development.

3. Empowering Others: Gentle leaders empower others to realize their full potential and contribute meaningfully to the collective vision. Like donkeys that encourage independence and initiative within their herd, leading with love involves recognizing and nurturing the unique talents and strengths of each individual, empowering them to take ownership of their roles and responsibilities.

4. Leading by Example: Leading with love requires leading by example—modeling the values, behaviors, and attitudes we wish to see in others. Like donkeys who exemplify patience, kindness, and resilience in their interactions, leading with love inspires trust, admiration, and loyalty among team members, fostering a culture of kindness, collaboration, and mutual support.

5. Cultivating Growth and Well-being: Gentle leaders prioritize the holistic well-being and growth of their team members, both professionally and personally. Like donkeys that prioritize the safety and welfare of their herd, leading with love involves creating a nurturing and inclusive environment where individuals feel supported in their journey of self-discovery and self-improvement.

Leading with love is about embracing empathy, compassion, and kindness as guiding principles in leadership. By drawing inspiration from the wisdom of donkeys and embodying qualities of presence, nurturing relationships, empowerment, leading by example, and cultivating growth and well-being, we can create workplaces and communities where love, trust, and collaboration flourish, enriching the lives of all who are touched by our leadership.

- Harnessing the Power of Compassionate Leadership

In the realm of leadership, compassion serves as a transformative force that fosters trust, collaboration, and collective success. Drawing inspiration from the innate wisdom of donkeys, this exploration delves into the principles of compassionate leadership and its profound impact on individuals, teams, and organizations.

1. Empathetic Understanding: Compassionate leadership begins with empathetic understanding—a deep appreciation of the thoughts, feelings, and experiences of others. Like donkeys that possess an innate ability to sense the emotions of their companions, compassionate leaders cultivate empathy and emotional intelligence, creating a safe and supportive space for individuals to express themselves authentically and feel understood.

2. Fostering Trust and Safety: Trust is the cornerstone of effective leadership, and compassion is its bedrock. Like donkeys that foster trust and cooperation within their herd through gentle guidance, compassionate leaders create a culture of trust and safety where individuals feel valued, respected, and supported in their endeavors. By leading with integrity, transparency, and authenticity, they inspire confidence and loyalty among team members, laying the foundation for collaborative success.

3. Cultivating Growth and Resilience: Compassionate leaders prioritize the growth and well-being of their team members, nurturing their potential and supporting them in times of challenge and adversity. Like donkeys that provide comfort and reassurance to their companions, compassionate leaders offer encouragement, mentorship, and resources to help individuals thrive and develop resilience in the face of obstacles. By fostering a culture of learning, innovation, and continuous improvement, they empower individuals to realize their full potential and contribute meaningfully to the collective mission.

4. Inspiring Purpose and Meaning: Compassionate leaders inspire purpose and meaning in their teams, aligning individual aspirations with the broader vision and values of the organization. Like donkeys who work together towards common goals with purpose and determination, compassionate leaders articulate a compelling vision that resonates with the hearts and minds of their team members, igniting passion, commitment, and a sense of belonging. By fostering a sense of purpose and significance in their work, they cultivate engagement, motivation, and fulfillment among team members, driving excellence and innovation in pursuit of shared objectives.

5. Embracing Diversity and Inclusion: Compassionate leaders embrace diversity and inclusion as sources of strength and innovation, honoring the unique perspectives, talents, and contributions of every individual. Like donkeys that value the diversity of their herd and recognize the strengths of each member, compassionate leaders create an inclusive environment where everyone feels welcome, respected, and valued for who they are. By fostering a culture of belonging and equity, they harness the collective wisdom and creativity of diverse teams, driving innovation and success through collaboration and mutual respect.

Compassionate leadership is a transformative force that fosters trust, collaboration, and collective well-being. By drawing inspiration from the innate wisdom of donkeys and embodying principles of empathetic understanding, trust-building, growth and resilience, purpose-driven leadership, and diversity and inclusion, we can cultivate cultures of compassion that enrich the lives of individuals, teams, and organizations, creating a brighter and more compassionate world for all.

Chapter 13: Community and Cooperation

In the intricate web of life, community and cooperation are the threads that bind individuals together, fostering connection, resilience, and collective well-being. Inspired by the harmonious dynamics of donkey herds, this chapter explores the principles of community and cooperation and their profound implications for building thriving communities and organizations.

1. Cultivating Connection: At the heart of community lies a deep sense of connection—a recognition of our interdependence and shared humanity. Like donkeys that form strong bonds within their herds, cultivating connection involves fostering relationships built on trust, empathy, and mutual respect. By nurturing authentic connections with others, we create a sense of belonging and support that strengthens the fabric of our communities and organizations.

2. Embracing Diversity: Diversity is the lifeblood of vibrant communities, enriching them with a tapestry of perspectives, talents, and experiences. Like donkeys that thrive in diverse herds, embracing diversity involves honoring the unique contributions of every individual and celebrating the richness of our differences. By creating inclusive spaces where everyone feels valued and respected, we harness the collective wisdom and creativity of diverse voices, driving innovation and progress.

3. Collaboration Over Competition: In a culture often defined by competition, collaboration emerges as a powerful antidote that fosters shared success and prosperity. Like donkeys that cooperate seamlessly within their herds to navigate challenges and opportunities, prioritizing collaboration involves transcending individual agendas in favor of collective goals. By fostering a culture of collaboration and teamwork, we amplify our collective impact and create pathways to shared prosperity and growth.

4. Mutual Support and Care: Community thrives on a foundation of mutual support and care—a commitment to uplifting and empowering one another in times of need. Like donkeys who offer comfort and protection to their companions, cultivating mutual support involves extending a helping hand, lending a listening ear, and providing encouragement and assistance when needed. By embodying the principles of compassion and solidarity, we create a culture of care that nurtures resilience and well-being for all.

5. Collective Responsibility: Building strong communities requires a shared commitment to collective responsibility—a recognition that we each have a role to play in shaping the world we want to inhabit. Like donkeys who work together to forage for food and navigate their environment, embracing collective responsibility involves taking ownership of our actions and their impact on others. By fostering a sense of stewardship and accountability, we co-create communities where everyone's needs are valued, and everyone has the opportunity to thrive.

Community and cooperation are the cornerstones of a thriving society, enriching our lives with connection, resilience, and collective well-being. By drawing inspiration from the harmonious dynamics of donkey herds and embodying principles of connection, diversity, collaboration, mutual support, and collective responsibility, we can create communities and organizations that reflect the best of humanity, where everyone has the opportunity to flourish and contribute to the greater good.

- **The Strength of Herds: Donkeys and the Importance of Community**

In the vast tapestry of nature, donkeys exemplify the power and resilience of community. This exploration delves into the profound lessons that donkeys teach us about the importance of community and the strength that arises from unity and cooperation.

1. Unity in Diversity: Donkey herds embody the beauty of diversity, with individuals of different ages, personalities, and abilities coming together as a cohesive unit. Like donkeys that thrive in diverse herds, communities flourish when they embrace and celebrate the richness of their differences. By honoring each member's unique strengths and contributions, communities harness the collective power of diversity to overcome challenges and achieve shared goals.

2. Mutual Support and Protection: In donkey herds, mutual support and protection are paramount, with individuals looking out for one another and offering assistance in times of need. Similarly, communities thrive when they foster a culture of solidarity and care, where members rally around each other in times of adversity and provide support and encouragement to help each other succeed. By cultivating a sense of belonging and interconnectedness, communities create a safety net that bolsters individual well-being and collective resilience.

3. Shared Resources and Responsibilities: Donkey herds operate on principles of shared resources and responsibilities, with individuals collaborating to forage for food, navigate their environment, and protect each other from threats. Likewise, communities function best when they recognize and honor their shared resources and responsibilities, working together to steward the environment, ensure equitable access to resources, and uphold the well-being of all members. By embracing collective stewardship and accountability, communities create a sustainable foundation for prosperity and harmony.

4. Collective Wisdom and Learning: Within donkey herds, collective wisdom and learning are passed down through generations, with older individuals imparting knowledge and experience to younger ones. Similarly, communities thrive when they value and prioritize lifelong learning and knowledge sharing, creating opportunities for intergenerational exchange and mentorship. By fostering a culture of curiosity and continuous growth, communities tap into the wealth of wisdom and innovation that arises from diverse perspectives and experiences.

5. Resilience in Adversity: Donkey herds demonstrate remarkable resilience in the face of adversity, weathering storms and overcoming challenges through unity and cooperation. Likewise, communities draw strength from their collective resilience, banding together to confront and overcome obstacles, whether natural disasters, economic hardships, or social injustices. By building networks of support and solidarity, communities emerge from adversity stronger and more united than ever, ready to face whatever challenges the future may bring.

Donkeys exemplify the power and beauty of community, teaching us valuable lessons about unity, diversity, mutual support, collective responsibility, and resilience. By drawing inspiration from the strength of donkey herds and embodying these principles in our own communities, we can create a world where everyone feels valued, supported, and empowered to thrive.

- **Fostering Collaboration and Cooperation in Human Society**

In the intricate tapestry of human society, collaboration and cooperation are the threads that weave together communities, organizations, and nations. Drawing inspiration from the harmonious dynamics of donkey herds, this exploration delves into strategies for fostering collaboration and cooperation in human society and unlocking the collective potential of diverse individuals and groups.

1. **Cultivating a Culture of Trust:** Trust serves as the foundation of collaboration, providing a safe and supportive environment where individuals feel empowered to share ideas, take risks, and work together towards common goals. Like donkeys that rely on trust and cooperation within their herd for survival, human society thrives when trust is nurtured through integrity, transparency, and open communication. By fostering trust in our interactions and institutions, we create a culture of collaboration where individuals feel valued, respected, and empowered to contribute their unique perspectives and talents.

2. **Embracing Diversity and Inclusion:** Diversity is a source of strength and innovation, enriching human society with a tapestry of perspectives, talents, and experiences. Like donkeys that thrive in diverse herds, human communities flourish when they embrace and celebrate the richness of their differences. By creating

inclusive spaces where everyone feels welcome, valued, and respected, we harness the collective wisdom and creativity of diverse individuals and groups, driving innovation and progress through collaboration and mutual respect.

3. Fostering Interconnectedness and Interdependence: Human society is inherently interconnected and interdependent, with individuals and communities relying on each other for support, resources, and mutual well-being. Like donkeys that collaborate seamlessly within their herd to navigate challenges and opportunities, fostering collaboration and cooperation involves recognizing and honoring our interconnectedness and interdependence. By building networks of support and solidarity, we create resilient communities that can weather storms and overcome obstacles together, emerging stronger and more united than ever.

4. Promoting Dialogue and Conflict Resolution: Effective collaboration requires open and constructive dialogue, where individuals listen actively, communicate honestly, and seek to understand each other's perspectives. Like donkeys who communicate through subtle cues and gestures to maintain harmony within their herd, human society benefits from respectful and empathetic communication that fosters understanding and empathy. By promoting dialogue and conflict resolution skills, we empower individuals and groups to navigate differences and disagreements constructively, finding common ground and forging solutions that benefit all.

5. Encouraging Shared Leadership and Collective Action: True collaboration involves shared leadership and collective action, with individuals working together towards shared goals and aspirations. Like donkeys who cooperate seamlessly within their herd to achieve common objectives, human society thrives when leadership is distributed, and individuals feel empowered to contribute their unique talents and strengths. By encouraging shared leadership and collective action, we tap into the collective potential of diverse individuals and groups, driving positive change and progress in our communities and beyond.

Fostering collaboration and cooperation in human society requires a commitment to building trust, embracing diversity and inclusion, recognizing our interconnectedness and interdependence, promoting dialogue and conflict resolution, and encouraging shared leadership and collective action. By drawing inspiration from the harmonious dynamics of donkey herds and embodying these principles in our interactions and institutions, we can create a world where collaboration flourishes, and all individuals have the opportunity to thrive and contribute to the greater good.

Chapter 14: Facing Challenges Head-On

Facing challenges head-on requires a combination of courage, determination, and resilience. In Chapter 14, we delve into the strategies and mindset needed to confront obstacles and adversities effectively.

1. Acknowledging the Challenge: The first step in facing any challenge is to acknowledge its existence. Denying or ignoring a problem only allows it to grow. By recognizing the challenge, you can begin to formulate a plan to overcome it.

2. Developing a Positive Mindset: Cultivating a positive mindset is crucial when facing challenges. Instead of focusing on the negative aspects, try to find opportunities for growth and learning. Viewing challenges as temporary hurdles rather than insurmountable obstacles can make them seem more manageable.

3. Setting Clear Goals: Establishing clear goals provides direction and motivation when facing challenges. Break down the larger challenge into smaller, achievable tasks, and set specific objectives for each one. This approach makes the challenge less overwhelming and allows you to track your progress along the way.

4. Seeking Support: Don't hesitate to seek support from friends, family, mentors, or colleagues when facing challenges. Talking about your concerns with others can provide valuable insights, encouragement, and perspective. Additionally, collaborating with others can generate new ideas and solutions to overcome the challenge.

5. Adapting to Change: Challenges often require flexibility and adaptation. Be prepared to adjust your strategies and approaches as needed. Embrace change as an opportunity for growth rather than a setback.

6. Learning from Failure: Failure is a natural part of facing challenges. Instead of letting it discourage you, use it as a learning experience. Analyze what went wrong, identify areas for improvement, and adjust your approach accordingly. Every setback brings an opportunity to grow stronger and wiser.

7. Maintaining Resilience: Resilience is the ability to bounce back from setbacks and adversity. Cultivate resilience by practicing self-care, maintaining a positive outlook, and staying connected to your support network. Remember that challenges are temporary, and with resilience, you can overcome them.

8. Celebrating Successes: Finally, don't forget to celebrate your successes along the way. Recognize and reward yourself for each milestone you achieve, no matter how small. Celebrating your progress boosts morale and reinforces your motivation to continue facing challenges head-on.

By embracing these strategies and adopting a proactive mindset, you can navigate challenges with confidence and emerge stronger on the other side. Remember, it's not the challenges themselves that define us, but how we choose to respond to them.

- Boldly Confronting Challenges: Lessons from Donkey Behavior

Drawing lessons from donkey behavior can offer valuable insights into boldly confronting challenges:

1. Stubborn Persistence: Donkeys are known for their stubborn persistence, often refusing to move when they sense danger or uncertainty. Similarly, when facing challenges, embracing a stubborn determination to persist can be beneficial. By refusing to give up at the first sign of difficulty, you can overcome obstacles with resilience and tenacity.

2. Practical Problem-Solving: Donkeys are intelligent animals that excel at practical problem-solving. They often find creative solutions to navigate difficult terrain or escape predators. Similarly, when confronted with challenges, adopting a practical and resourceful approach can lead to innovative solutions. Rather than becoming overwhelmed by the complexity of the problem, break it down into manageable steps and explore different strategies to overcome it.

3. Independent Thinking: Donkeys are independent creatures that prefer to think for themselves rather than blindly following others. When facing challenges, it's essential to trust your instincts and rely on your own judgment. While seeking advice and support from others is valuable, ultimately, you must make decisions that align with your goals and values.

4. Adaptability: Donkeys are highly adaptable animals that can thrive in diverse environments. They can adjust their behavior and strategies to suit changing circumstances. Similarly, when confronting challenges, being adaptable and flexible is key to success. Recognize that not every approach will work, and be willing to adapt your tactics as needed to overcome obstacles effectively.

5. Resilience in the Face of Adversity: Donkeys are resilient animals that can endure harsh conditions and overcome adversity. When facing challenges, cultivating resilience is essential. Embrace setbacks as opportunities for growth, and remain steadfast in your determination to persevere despite obstacles.

By drawing inspiration from the behavior of donkeys, individuals can learn valuable lessons about boldly confronting challenges with persistence, practical problem-solving, independent thinking, adaptability, and resilience.

- Building Courage and Tenacity in the Face of Adversity

Building courage and tenacity in the face of adversity is a transformative journey that requires dedication and self-reflection. Here are some strategies to cultivate these qualities:

1. Embrace Fear: Courage isn't the absence of fear but the ability to act despite it. Acknowledge your fears and confront them head-on. By facing your fears, you gradually build resilience and confidence in your ability to overcome challenges.

2. Set Bold Goals: Challenge yourself by setting ambitious goals that push you out of your comfort zone. Break these goals down into smaller, manageable steps, and celebrate your progress along the way. Each accomplishment reinforces your belief in your capabilities.

3. Learn from Setbacks: Instead of viewing setbacks as failures, see them as opportunities for growth. Reflect on what went wrong and identify lessons learned. Use these insights to adjust your approach and move forward with renewed determination.

4. Seek Support: Surround yourself with a supportive network of friends, family, mentors, and peers who encourage and uplift you during difficult times. Lean on them for guidance, advice, and encouragement when facing challenges.

5. Practice Self-Compassion: Treat yourself with kindness and compassion, especially when things don't go as planned. Avoid self-criticism and negative self-talk, and instead, focus on nurturing a positive and empowering inner dialogue.

6. Visualize Success: Use visualization techniques to imagine yourself overcoming challenges and achieving your goals. Visualizing success can help build confidence and motivation, making it easier to stay committed to your objectives.

7. Stay Persistent: Tenacity is the ability to persist in the face of adversity. Develop a "never give up" mindset and remain committed to your goals, even when the going gets tough. Remember that setbacks are temporary, and with perseverance, you can overcome any obstacle.

8. Celebrate Achievements: Celebrate your successes, no matter how small. Recognize and reward yourself for your accomplishments, as this reinforces positive behavior and boosts morale.

9. Stay Flexible: While persistence is essential, it's also crucial to remain flexible and adaptable in your approach. Be open to new ideas and solutions, and be willing to pivot when necessary to navigate unforeseen challenges.

10. Practice Courageous Action: Take intentional steps outside of your comfort zone on a regular basis. Whether it's speaking up in a meeting, trying a new hobby, or pursuing a long-held dream, each act of courage strengthens your resilience and confidence.

By incorporating these strategies into your life, you can gradually build courage and tenacity, empowering yourself to face adversity with resilience and determination.

Chapter 15: Resilience in the Face of Criticism

Criticism is an inevitable part of life, but how we respond to it determines our resilience and growth. In this chapter, we explore strategies for cultivating resilience in the face of criticism.

1. Understand the Source: Criticism can come from various sources, including peers, supervisors, or even strangers. Understanding the source of criticism can provide valuable context and help determine its validity. Consider the intentions and motivations behind the critique before internalizing it.

2. Separate Feedback from Self-Worth: It's essential to separate feedback on your actions or behavior from your intrinsic self-worth. Criticism of your work or decisions does not diminish your value as a person. Remind yourself of your strengths and accomplishments to maintain a healthy sense of self-esteem.

3. Focus on Growth: Instead of viewing criticism as a personal attack, reframe it as an opportunity for growth and improvement. Embrace a growth mindset, where challenges and feedback are seen as opportunities to learn and develop. Use criticism constructively to identify areas for growth and refine your skills.

4. Seek Constructive Feedback: Not all criticism is created equal. Seek out constructive feedback from trusted mentors, peers, or supervisors who have your best interests at heart. Constructive criticism is specific, actionable, and focused on helping you improve.

5. Respond Calmly and Professionally: When faced with criticism, respond calmly and professionally. Avoid reacting defensively or emotionally, as this can escalate the situation and hinder constructive dialogue. Instead, take a step back, listen actively, and consider the feedback thoughtfully before responding.

6. Learn to Let Go: Not all criticism will be valid or constructive. Learning to discern between helpful feedback and baseless criticism is essential for maintaining resilience. Recognize that you cannot control others' opinions or perceptions and focus on what you can control—your actions and reactions.

7. Practice Self-Compassion: Be kind to yourself when facing criticism. Practice self-compassion by treating yourself with the same understanding and kindness you would offer a friend in a similar situation. Remind yourself that making mistakes and receiving criticism are natural parts of the learning and growth process.

8. Build a Support Network: Surround yourself with a supportive network of friends, family, and colleagues who uplift and encourage you during challenging times. Lean on them for guidance, perspective, and emotional support when facing criticism.

9. Maintain Perspective: Keep criticism in perspective by considering the bigger picture. One negative comment or critique does not define your worth or abilities. Focus on your long-term goals and aspirations, and don't let temporary setbacks derail your progress.

10. Celebrate Resilience: Finally, celebrate your resilience in the face of criticism. Recognize your ability to withstand adversity, learn from feedback, and emerge stronger and more resilient than before. Each experience of criticism is an opportunity to grow and develop as a person.

By embracing these strategies, you can cultivate resilience in the face of criticism, turning challenges into opportunities for growth and self-improvement. Remember that resilience is not about avoiding criticism altogether but about facing it with courage, grace, and a willingness to learn.

- Thick Skin and Tender Hearts: Donkeys and Dealing with Criticism

Drawing inspiration from donkeys, we can learn valuable lessons about dealing with criticism while maintaining both resilience and compassion:

1. Thick Skin: Donkeys possess thick hides that offer protection against external elements and predators. Similarly, developing a "thick skin" can help shield us from the sting of criticism. By cultivating resilience and confidence in ourselves and our abilities, we can withstand negative feedback without allowing it to undermine our self-worth.

2. Tender Hearts: Despite their tough exteriors, donkeys are known for their gentle and empathetic nature. Similarly, it's essential to maintain a "tender heart" when receiving criticism. Approach feedback with an open mind and a willingness to listen and understand the perspective of the critic. Responding with empathy and compassion can foster constructive dialogue and mutual respect.

3. Steadfastness: Donkeys are steadfast animals, known for their unwavering determination and perseverance. When facing criticism, embodying this steadfastness can help us stay grounded in our values and convictions. Rather than allowing criticism to sway us from our path, we can remain resolute in our beliefs and continue to pursue our goals with confidence.

4. Selective Listening: Donkeys are discerning animals that carefully filter out irrelevant noise and distractions. Similarly, when receiving criticism, it's essential to practice selective listening. Discern which feedback is constructive and actionable, worthy of consideration and potential implementation, and which is simply unhelpful or malicious. Focus your attention on the feedback that has the potential to facilitate growth and improvement.

5. Adaptability: Donkeys are highly adaptable creatures, capable of thriving in diverse environments and situations. Similarly, when confronted with criticism, it's essential to embrace adaptability. Use feedback as an opportunity to reflect on your actions and behaviors, and be willing to adapt and evolve as needed. Flexibility and a willingness to learn from criticism can foster personal and professional growth.

6. Respectful Boundaries: Donkeys are known for their strong sense of boundaries and self-preservation. Similarly, it's crucial to establish and maintain respectful boundaries when receiving criticism. Set clear boundaries around what feedback is acceptable and constructive, and communicate these boundaries assertively but respectfully. Upholding these boundaries can help preserve your well-being and self-esteem while still allowing for open dialogue and growth.

By embodying the qualities of donkeys—thick skin, tender hearts, steadfastness, selective listening, adaptability, and respectful boundaries—we can navigate criticism with resilience, empathy, and grace. Ultimately, dealing with criticism is not about shutting ourselves off from feedback but about cultivating a balanced approach that allows us to learn and grow while staying true to ourselves.

- Developing Resilience in Times of Judgment and Doubt

Developing resilience in times of judgment and doubt is a transformative process that requires self-awareness, self-compassion, and proactive strategies. Here's how you can cultivate resilience when facing criticism or self-doubt:

1. Self-Reflection: Take time to reflect on your thoughts, feelings, and reactions to criticism or doubt. Understand your triggers and how they impact your resilience. Self-awareness is the first step towards building resilience.

2. Challenge Negative Thoughts: Practice cognitive reframing to challenge negative thoughts and beliefs about yourself. Instead of internalizing criticism or succumbing to self-doubt, reframe negative thoughts into more positive and empowering statements.

3. Focus on Strengths: Shift your focus from perceived weaknesses to your strengths and accomplishments. Remind yourself of past successes and the skills and qualities that make you resilient. Celebrate your achievements, no matter how small.

4. Set Realistic Goals: Break larger goals into smaller, achievable tasks. Setting realistic goals allows you to make progress despite setbacks and boosts your confidence along the way. Celebrate each milestone as you work towards your objectives.

5. Practice Self-Compassion: Treat yourself with kindness and understanding, especially during times of judgment or doubt. Practice self-compassion by offering yourself the same warmth and support you would offer a friend in a similar situation. Validate your emotions and remind yourself that it's okay to make mistakes or feel uncertain.

6. Seek Support: Reach out to supportive friends, family members, or mentors who can offer encouragement and perspective during challenging times. Sharing your feelings with trusted individuals can help you feel less isolated and provide valuable insights into managing criticism and doubt.

7. Learn from Challenges: View challenges, criticism, and self-doubt as opportunities for growth and learning. Embrace setbacks as valuable lessons that contribute to your personal and professional development. Use feedback constructively to identify areas for improvement and refine your skills.

8. Practice Resilience-Building Activities: Engage in activities that promote resilience, such as mindfulness meditation, journaling, exercise, or creative expression. These activities can help reduce stress, increase self-awareness, and cultivate a sense of inner strength and calm.

9. Maintain Perspective: Remember that criticism and self-doubt are temporary experiences that do not define your worth or potential. Keep things in perspective by focusing on the bigger picture and your long-term goals. Trust in your ability to overcome challenges and persevere in the face of adversity.

10. Celebrate Progress: Acknowledge and celebrate your progress, no matter how small. Recognize the efforts you're making to build resilience and manage judgment and doubt effectively. Each step forward is a testament to your strength and resilience.

By incorporating these strategies into your life, you can develop resilience in times of judgment and doubt, empowering yourself to navigate challenges with confidence, self-compassion, and determination.

Chapter 16: Living in Harmony with Nature

Living in harmony with nature is not only essential for the well-being of the planet but also for our own physical, mental, and emotional health. In this chapter, we explore the importance of reconnecting with nature and practical ways to live more sustainably.

1. Reconnecting with Nature: In today's fast-paced world, it's easy to become disconnected from the natural world. However, spending time in nature has been shown to reduce stress, improve mood, and enhance overall well-being. Whether it's a walk in the park, gardening, or simply sitting outdoors, prioritize activities that allow you to connect with the beauty and tranquility of nature.

2. Cultivating Sustainability: Adopting sustainable practices in our daily lives is crucial for preserving the health of the planet for future generations. Reduce your carbon footprint by conserving energy, minimizing waste, and choosing environmentally friendly products and transportation options. Small changes in habits can have a significant impact when multiplied across communities and societies.

3. Respecting Biodiversity: Biodiversity is essential for maintaining healthy ecosystems and the balance of life on Earth. Support conservation efforts by protecting natural habitats, promoting wildlife-friendly practices, and advocating for policies that preserve biodiversity.

Recognize the intrinsic value of all living beings and strive to coexist harmoniously with the diverse species that share our planet.

4. Practicing Mindfulness: Mindfulness involves paying attention to the present moment with openness and curiosity. Incorporate mindfulness practices into your daily routine, such as meditation, yoga, or mindful walking in nature. Cultivating awareness of our interconnectedness with the natural world can foster a deeper appreciation and respect for the environment.

5. Promoting Sustainable Agriculture: The food we eat has a significant impact on the environment. Support local, organic, and sustainable food producers who prioritize ethical and environmentally friendly farming practices. Consider reducing meat consumption and incorporating more plant-based foods into your diet, which requires fewer resources and generates less pollution.

6. Conserving Resources: Conserve natural resources such as water, soil, and forests by adopting responsible consumption habits. Reduce water usage, practice soil conservation techniques, and support reforestation efforts to replenish and protect vital ecosystems. Remember that every action we take has the potential to contribute to the preservation or degradation of the environment.

7. Educating and Inspiring Others: Share your knowledge and passion for living in harmony with nature with others. Educate friends, family, and community members about the importance of environmental stewardship and inspire them to take action. By collectively working towards a more sustainable future, we can create positive change on a global scale.

8. Advocating for Environmental Justice: Environmental justice involves addressing the disproportionate impact of environmental degradation on marginalized communities. Stand up for the rights of those most affected by pollution, climate change, and ecological destruction. Advocate for policies and initiatives that promote equitable access to clean air, water, and natural resources for all people, regardless of race, ethnicity, or socioeconomic status.

By embracing these principles and practices, we can cultivate a deeper connection with nature, promote sustainability, and contribute to the well-being of both the planet and ourselves. Living in harmony with nature is not only a responsibility but also a source of joy, inspiration, and fulfillment.

- Donkeys and the Rhythms of Nature: A Lesson in Harmony

Drawing inspiration from donkeys and the rhythms of nature, we can learn valuable lessons about living in harmony with the natural world:

1. Respecting Natural Cycles: Donkeys, like many animals, are attuned to the natural rhythms of the environment. They graze, rest, and seek shelter in accordance with the cycles of day and night, seasons, and weather patterns. Similarly, living in harmony with nature involves respecting these natural cycles and adapting our activities and lifestyles accordingly. By aligning our behavior with the rhythms of nature, we can enhance our well-being and minimize our impact on the environment.

2. Simplicity and Minimalism: Donkeys lead simple lives, relying on basic necessities such as food, water, and shelter. Their minimalist lifestyle teaches us the value of simplicity and the importance of living in balance with our surroundings. Embracing a more minimalist lifestyle can reduce consumption and waste, leading to a lighter ecological footprint and a greater sense of harmony with the natural world.

3. Connection to the Land: Donkeys have a deep connection to the land, rooted in their history as working animals in rural landscapes. They remind us of the importance of cultivating a connection to the land and appreciating the beauty and abundance of the natural world. Spending time outdoors, gardening, or participating in conservation activities can deepen our connection to the land and foster a sense of stewardship for the Earth.

4. Embracing Slow Living: Donkeys are known for their unhurried pace and patient demeanor. In a world characterized by busyness and constant activity, they offer a powerful reminder to embrace slow living and savor the present moment. Slowing down allows us to appreciate the beauty of nature, cultivate mindfulness, and nurture our relationships with others and the environment.

5. Community and Cooperation: Donkeys are social animals that thrive in the company of others. They demonstrate the importance of community and cooperation in navigating the challenges of life. Building strong connections with our communities and working together towards common goals fosters a sense of solidarity and mutual support, strengthening our collective ability to live in harmony with nature.

6. Resilience and Adaptability: Donkeys are known for their resilience and adaptability, able to thrive in a variety of environments and conditions. They teach us the importance of resilience in the face of change and adversity. By cultivating resilience and adaptability, we can better navigate the challenges posed by environmental degradation, climate change, and other threats to the natural world.

7. Appreciation for Simple Pleasures: Finally, donkeys remind us to appreciate the simple pleasures of life—the feel of the sun on our backs, the taste of fresh grass, the sound of birdsong. In a world filled with distractions and complexities, they encourage us to slow down, be present, and find joy in the beauty of the natural world.

By embracing these lessons from donkeys and the rhythms of nature, we can cultivate a deeper sense of harmony with the Earth and foster a more sustainable and fulfilling way of life.

- Cultivating Eco-consciousness and Sustainability

Cultivating eco-consciousness and sustainability involves adopting mindful practices and making conscious choices that minimize our environmental impact and promote the health and well-being of the planet. Here are some ways to cultivate eco-consciousness and sustainability in your daily life:

1. Reduce, Reuse, Recycle: Embrace the "three Rs" of sustainability by reducing waste, reusing items whenever possible, and recycling materials to minimize landfill waste and conserve resources.

2. Conserve Energy: Reduce your energy consumption by turning off lights and electronics when not in use, using energy-efficient appliances and light bulbs, and maximizing natural light and ventilation in your home.

3. Conserve Water: Practice water conservation by fixing leaks, taking shorter showers, using water-efficient appliances, and watering outdoor plants during the cooler parts of the day to minimize evaporation.

4. Choose Sustainable Transportation: Opt for eco-friendly transportation options such as walking, cycling, carpooling, or using public transportation to reduce carbon emissions and air pollution from fossil fuel-powered vehicles.

5. Support Sustainable Agriculture: Choose locally grown, organic, and sustainably produced foods whenever possible to reduce the environmental impact of food production, support local farmers, and promote biodiversity.

6. Reduce Meat Consumption: Limiting your consumption of meat and dairy products can significantly reduce your carbon footprint, as animal agriculture is a major contributor to greenhouse gas emissions and deforestation.

7. Shop Responsibly: Support companies and brands that prioritize sustainability and ethical practices in their production processes. Look for eco-friendly certifications, such as Fair Trade, USDA Organic, or Forest Stewardship Council (FSC) certification, when making purchasing decisions.

8. Minimize Single-Use Plastics: Reduce your use of single-use plastics such as plastic bags, bottles, and straws by opting for reusable alternatives or choosing products with minimal packaging.

9. Practice Mindful Consumption: Before making a purchase, consider whether you truly need the item and its environmental impact. Choose high-quality, durable products that are designed to last and repair rather than replace items whenever possible.

10. Get Involved: Engage in environmental advocacy and activism by supporting organizations and initiatives that promote sustainability, conservation, and climate action. Participate in community clean-up events, tree plantings, or environmental education programs to make a positive impact in your local area.

By incorporating these practices into your daily life and fostering a mindset of eco-consciousness and sustainability, you can contribute to a healthier planet and inspire others to do the same. Remember that even small actions can make a big difference when multiplied across individuals and communities.

Chapter 17: Embracing Individuality

Embracing individuality is a celebration of diversity and self-expression. In this chapter, we explore the importance of honoring our unique identities and the benefits of fostering a culture of acceptance and inclusion.

1. Celebrating Diversity: Diversity enriches our lives by bringing a variety of perspectives, experiences, and talents to the table. Embrace the uniqueness of individuals from different backgrounds, cultures, and identities, recognizing that diversity is a source of strength and innovation.

2. Honoring Authenticity: Authenticity involves living in alignment with our true selves, free from the constraints of societal expectations or conformity. Embrace your authentic self and encourage others to do the same, creating a space where individuals feel empowered to express their true identities without fear of judgment or rejection.

3. Respecting Differences: Respect differences in opinion, belief, and lifestyle, recognizing that everyone has their own journey and perspective. Foster open-mindedness and empathy, seeking to understand and appreciate the experiences and perspectives of others, even when they differ from our own.

4. Challenging Stereotypes: Challenge stereotypes and prejudices that limit the potential of individuals based on characteristics such as race, gender, sexual orientation, or ability. Advocate for equality and justice, promoting a society where everyone has the opportunity to thrive regardless of societal norms or expectations.

5. Encouraging Self-Expression: Encourage self-expression and creativity in all its forms, whether through art, music, fashion, or personal interests. Create environments that support individuality and self-discovery, where individuals feel free to explore and express their unique talents and passions.

6. Fostering Inclusion: Foster a sense of belonging and inclusion by creating spaces that are welcoming and inclusive of all individuals, regardless of their background or identity. Take proactive steps to address barriers to participation and ensure that everyone feels valued and respected.

7. Empowering Authentic Leadership: Cultivate authentic leadership that values transparency, integrity, and inclusivity. Encourage leaders to lead by example, embracing their own individuality and empowering others to do the same. Authentic leaders inspire trust and loyalty by staying true to themselves and their values.

8. Building Community: Build community and connection by creating opportunities for meaningful interaction and collaboration among individuals from diverse backgrounds. Foster a sense of camaraderie and mutual support, where everyone feels seen, heard, and valued for who they are.

9. Promoting Self-Acceptance: Promote self-acceptance and self-love by encouraging individuals to embrace their strengths, quirks, and imperfections. Challenge unrealistic beauty standards and societal norms that promote conformity over authenticity, affirming that everyone is worthy of love and respect just as they are.

10. Inspiring Change: Use your voice and platform to inspire positive change in the world, advocating for a society that celebrates and uplifts individuality in all its forms. Be a catalyst for progress and transformation, working towards a future where everyone can live authentically and fully embrace their unique identities.

By embracing individuality and fostering a culture of acceptance and inclusion, we can create a world where everyone feels empowered to be their true selves and contribute their unique gifts to the collective tapestry of humanity.

- Celebrating Uniqueness: Donkeys and the Beauty of Diversity

Celebrating uniqueness is akin to acknowledging the beauty of diversity, and donkeys offer insightful lessons in this regard:

1. Distinctive Physical Traits: Donkeys come in various shapes, sizes, and colors, showcasing the diversity within their species. Similarly, celebrating uniqueness involves appreciating the individual characteristics and traits that make each person special. Just as donkeys vary in appearance, people possess their own unique physical attributes that contribute to their beauty and identity.

2. Varied Personalities: Donkeys exhibit a wide range of personalities, from outgoing and friendly to shy and reserved. Similarly, people have diverse personalities, interests, and quirks that make them distinct individuals. Celebrating uniqueness means embracing the differences in temperament, preferences, and behavior that contribute to the richness of human experience.

3. Adaptability to Environment: Donkeys are highly adaptable animals, capable of thriving in diverse environments and climates. Similarly, people demonstrate resilience and adaptability in navigating the complexities of life. Celebrating uniqueness involves recognizing the strengths and abilities that allow individuals to adapt and flourish in various circumstances.

4. Contributions to Community: Donkeys play essential roles in agriculture, transportation, and therapy, highlighting their value to human communities. Similarly, each person has their own talents, skills, and contributions to offer to society. Celebrating uniqueness means acknowledging and valuing the diverse abilities and contributions of individuals within our communities.

5. Strength in Unity: Donkeys often live in herds or pairs, relying on each other for companionship and support. Similarly, people find strength and unity in embracing diversity and inclusion. Celebrating uniqueness involves fostering a sense of community and solidarity that values and respects the differences among individuals.

6. Appreciation of Heritage: Donkeys have a rich cultural and historical significance, playing roles in various civilizations and traditions around the world. Similarly, people have diverse cultural backgrounds, histories, and traditions that shape their identities. Celebrating uniqueness involves honoring and preserving the cultural heritage and diversity of individuals and communities.

7. Ecosystem Harmony: Donkeys contribute to the ecological balance of their habitats through grazing and soil management. Similarly, people have a responsibility to steward and protect the natural environment. Celebrating uniqueness includes recognizing the interconnectedness of all living beings and promoting environmental conservation and sustainability.

By celebrating uniqueness, we honor the beauty of diversity in all its forms, recognizing the intrinsic value and worth of every individual. Just as donkeys contribute to the richness of ecosystems with their diversity, people enrich the fabric of society with their unique talents, perspectives, and experiences.

- **Embracing Individuality and Authenticity in Human Life**

Embracing individuality and authenticity in human life is a journey of self-discovery, self-acceptance, and self-expression. Here's how you can cultivate these qualities:

1. Know Yourself: Take time to explore your interests, values, strengths, and weaknesses. Self-awareness is the foundation of authenticity, allowing you to understand who you are and what you stand for.

2. Be True to Yourself: Embrace your unique identity and values, even if they differ from societal norms or expectations. Authenticity involves staying true to yourself and living in alignment with your beliefs and principles.

3. Express Yourself: Find creative outlets for self-expression, whether through art, music, writing, or other forms of creative expression. Expressing yourself authentically allows you to share your unique perspective with the world.

4. Set Boundaries: Establish healthy boundaries that honor your needs, values, and limits. Boundaries are essential for protecting your authenticity and preserving your sense of self in relationships and interactions with others.

5. Practice Self-Compassion: Be kind and compassionate towards yourself, especially during times of self-doubt or insecurity. Practice self-compassion by treating yourself with the same understanding and kindness you would offer a friend in a similar situation.

6. Embrace Imperfection: Accept that no one is perfect, and that making mistakes is a natural part of the human experience. Embracing imperfection allows you to let go of unrealistic expectations and embrace your authentic self.

7. Surround Yourself with Supportive People: Surround yourself with people who accept and support you for who you are, without judgment or criticism. Cultivate relationships that celebrate your individuality and encourage you to be your authentic self.

8. Seek Growth and Development: Strive for personal growth and development, while staying true to your core values and beliefs. Authenticity involves a willingness to learn, grow, and evolve while remaining grounded in who you are.

9. Lead by Example: Be an authentic role model for others by living your life with integrity, honesty, and authenticity. Your example can inspire others to embrace their own individuality and authenticity.

10. Celebrate Diversity: Appreciate the diversity of human experience and celebrate the unique qualities and perspectives that each individual brings to the table. Embracing diversity enriches our communities and fosters a culture of acceptance and inclusion.

By embracing individuality and authenticity in human life, we honor the uniqueness of each person and create a world where everyone feels empowered to be their true selves.

Chapter 18: The Gift of Contentment

Contentment is a state of inner peace and satisfaction that comes from appreciating what we have and finding joy in the present moment. In this chapter, we explore the importance of cultivating contentment and practical ways to find happiness and fulfillment in our lives.

1. Gratitude Practice: Cultivate a daily gratitude practice by reflecting on the things you're thankful for, both big and small. Gratitude shifts your focus from what you lack to what you have, fostering a sense of contentment and abundance.

2. Mindfulness Meditation: Practice mindfulness meditation to cultivate awareness of the present moment and develop a non-judgmental attitude towards your thoughts and feelings. Mindfulness helps you appreciate life's simple pleasures and find contentment in the here and now.

3. Savoring Life's Joys: Slow down and savor life's moments of joy and beauty, whether it's a breathtaking sunset, a delicious meal, or a heartfelt conversation with a loved one. Savoring enhances your enjoyment of life and deepens your sense of contentment.

4. Finding Fulfillment in Relationships: Invest time and energy in nurturing meaningful relationships with friends, family, and loved ones. Strong social connections provide a sense of belonging and support, contributing to overall happiness and contentment.

5. Setting Realistic Expectations: Manage your expectations by setting realistic goals and priorities that align with your values and aspirations. Unrealistic expectations can lead to disappointment and dissatisfaction, while realistic goals promote a sense of accomplishment and contentment.

6. Practicing Self-Compassion: Be kind and compassionate towards yourself, especially during challenging times or moments of self-doubt. Practice self-care and self-compassion by treating yourself with the same kindness and understanding you would offer to a friend in need.

7. Living in Alignment with Values: Align your actions and choices with your core values and beliefs, living a life that feels authentic and meaningful to you. When your actions are in alignment with your values, you experience a deeper sense of purpose and contentment.

8. Embracing Imperfection: Accept that life is full of imperfections and uncertainties, and that it's okay not to have everything figured out. Embracing imperfection allows you to let go of unrealistic standards and find contentment in the midst of life's challenges.

9. Cultivating Inner Peace: Develop practices that promote inner peace and emotional well-being, such as yoga, deep breathing exercises, or spending time in nature. Cultivating inner peace helps you navigate life's ups and downs with grace and equanimity.

10. Giving Back to Others: Find fulfillment and contentment in giving back to others through acts of kindness, volunteering, or supporting causes you're passionate about. Giving back fosters a sense of connection and purpose, enriching both your life and the lives of others.

By cultivating contentment in our lives, we can experience greater happiness, fulfillment, and peace of mind. Contentment is not about seeking external validation or material wealth but about finding joy and satisfaction in the present moment, exactly as it is.

- Contentment in Stillness: Donkeys and the Art of Being Present

Contentment in stillness is a concept that draws inspiration from the serene nature of donkeys and their ability to embody presence. Here's how we can learn from donkeys and cultivate contentment in stillness:

1. Embracing Silence: Donkeys often exude a sense of tranquility in their quiet moments. Similarly, finding contentment in stillness involves embracing moments of silence and solitude, allowing ourselves to disconnect from the noise of the world and simply be present with ourselves.

2. Being Mindful of the Present: Donkeys are masters of living in the moment, fully engaged in their surroundings without distraction. Practicing mindfulness allows us to cultivate a similar sense of presence, focusing our attention on the here and now with openness and curiosity.

3. Appreciating Simple Pleasures: Donkeys find contentment in simple pleasures, such as grazing in a sunlit pasture or feeling a gentle breeze against their skin. Similarly, we can find joy and satisfaction in life's small moments of beauty and wonder, appreciating the simple pleasures that surround us each day.

4. Connecting with Nature: Donkeys have a deep connection to nature, thriving in outdoor environments where they can graze and roam freely. Spending time in nature allows us to reconnect with our natural surroundings, fostering a sense of calm and contentment in the midst of the natural world's beauty.

5. Letting Go of Distractions: Donkeys are adept at tuning out distractions and staying grounded in the present moment. Similarly, cultivating contentment in stillness involves letting go of distractions and mental clutter, allowing ourselves to fully immerse in the present moment without judgment or attachment.

6. Finding Solace in Solitude: Donkeys are solitary creatures by nature, often finding solace in moments of solitude. Similarly, we can find contentment in stillness by embracing periods of solitude as opportunities for self-reflection, introspection, and inner peace.

7. Savoring Moments of Rest: Donkeys know the importance of rest and relaxation, often taking leisurely naps or basking in the warmth of the sun. Similarly, finding contentment in stillness involves savoring moments of rest and relaxation, allowing ourselves to recharge and rejuvenate our minds, bodies, and spirits.

8. Embracing Non-Doing: Donkeys are comfortable with simply being, without the need for constant activity or productivity. Similarly, finding contentment in stillness involves embracing the concept of non-doing, letting go of the pressure to constantly achieve or accomplish and allowing ourselves to simply exist in the present moment.

By learning from the gentle nature of donkeys and embracing the art of being present, we can cultivate a deeper sense of contentment in stillness, finding peace and fulfillment in the simple moments of life.

- Finding Fulfillment in the Here and Now

Finding fulfillment in the here and now is a transformative practice that involves embracing the present moment with gratitude and openness. Here's how you can cultivate a sense of fulfillment in the here and now:

1. Practice Mindfulness: Cultivate mindfulness by paying attention to the present moment with curiosity and non-judgment. Engage your senses fully in your surroundings, noticing the sights, sounds, smells, tastes, and textures of the present moment. Mindfulness allows you to appreciate the richness of life as it unfolds moment by moment.

2. Gratitude Attitude: Cultivate an attitude of gratitude by focusing on the blessings and abundance in your life. Take time each day to reflect on the things you're thankful for, whether it's a supportive friend, a beautiful sunset, or a warm cup of tea. Gratitude shifts your focus from what you lack to what you have, fostering a sense of contentment and fulfillment.

3. Embrace Impermanence: Recognize the impermanent nature of life and savor each moment as it arises. Embracing impermanence allows you to let go of attachments to the past or worries about the future, and fully immerse yourself in the present moment. Every moment is precious and fleeting, so make the most of it while it lasts.

4. Find Joy in Simple Pleasures: Seek out and savor life's simple pleasures, whether it's enjoying a delicious meal, spending time with loved ones, or taking a leisurely walk in nature. Finding joy in simple pleasures cultivates a sense of fulfillment and contentment in the present moment.

5. Set Meaningful Intentions: Set intentions for how you want to show up in the world and live your life with purpose and meaning. Align your actions with your values and aspirations, and strive to make a positive impact on the lives of others. Living with intentionality allows you to live more fully in the here and now, with clarity and purpose.

6. Practice Acceptance and Letting Go: Acceptance involves acknowledging and embracing the reality of the present moment, without resistance or judgment. Let go of the need to control or change things that are beyond your control, and instead focus on responding with wisdom and compassion. Acceptance frees you to fully experience life as it unfolds, without being hindered by attachment or aversion.

7. Cultivate Presence in Relationships: Be fully present in your interactions with others, listening deeply and offering your full attention without distraction. Cultivating presence in relationships fosters deeper connections and enhances the quality of your interactions, leading to greater fulfillment and satisfaction in your social connections.

8. Practice Self-Compassion: Be kind and compassionate towards yourself, especially during times of difficulty or challenge. Treat yourself with the same warmth and understanding you would offer to a friend in need, and practice self-care to nurture your physical, emotional, and spiritual well-being. Self-compassion allows you to find fulfillment in the here and now, regardless of external circumstances.

By incorporating these practices into your life, you can cultivate a deeper sense of fulfillment and contentment in the present moment, leading to greater happiness and well-being overall.

Chapter 19: Lessons in Forgiveness and Compassion

Forgiveness and compassion are powerful practices that have the ability to transform our lives and relationships. In this chapter, we explore the importance of forgiveness and compassion, and the valuable lessons they teach us:

1. Letting Go of Resentment: Forgiveness involves releasing resentment and anger towards ourselves and others for past hurts or transgressions. By letting go of grudges and resentment, we free ourselves from the burden of carrying negative emotions and find peace and healing in our hearts.

2. Healing Wounds: Forgiveness is a healing balm that can mend emotional wounds and restore broken relationships. When we forgive others, we open the door to reconciliation and repair, allowing for greater understanding, empathy, and connection.

3. Cultivating Empathy: Compassion is the ability to empathize with the suffering of others and respond with kindness and understanding. By cultivating empathy, we deepen our connections with others and foster a sense of solidarity and support in our communities.

4. Breaking the Cycle of Hurt: Forgiveness and compassion break the cycle of hurt and retaliation, replacing it with understanding and reconciliation.

Instead of perpetuating conflict and resentment, forgiveness and compassion pave the way for healing and transformation.

5. Releasing Inner Peace: Forgiveness and compassion lead to inner peace and emotional freedom. When we forgive ourselves and others, we release the grip of negative emotions and find serenity and acceptance within ourselves.

6. Fostering Self-Compassion: Self-forgiveness and self-compassion are essential aspects of forgiveness and compassion. By extending kindness and understanding to ourselves, we cultivate a sense of self-worth and acceptance that allows us to move forward with grace and resilience.

7. Choosing Love Over Judgment: Forgiveness and compassion require us to choose love over judgment, understanding over condemnation. By seeing the humanity in others and ourselves, we open our hearts to the possibility of reconciliation and healing.

8. Embracing Imperfection: Forgiveness and compassion acknowledge the inherent imperfection of being human. By embracing our own imperfections and the imperfections of others, we create space for growth, forgiveness, and transformation.

9. Nurturing Gratitude: Forgiveness and compassion cultivate gratitude for the opportunities for growth and connection that arise from challenging situations. By seeing the silver lining in adversity, we find meaning and purpose in our experiences.

10. Spreading Kindness: Forgiveness and compassion inspire acts of kindness and generosity towards others. By extending forgiveness and compassion to others, we create a ripple effect of love and positivity that uplifts and transforms our world.

By embracing the lessons of forgiveness and compassion, we can cultivate deeper connections, heal emotional wounds, and create a world where love and understanding prevail.

- Forgiveness Unbridled: Donkeys and the Power of Letting Go

Drawing inspiration from donkeys, we can learn valuable lessons about the power of forgiveness and the art of letting go:

1. Release of Burdens: Donkeys are known for their strength and resilience, but they also symbolize the ability to carry heavy loads. Similarly, forgiveness allows us to release the burdens of anger, resentment, and hurt that weighs us down. By letting go of grudges and grievances, we lighten our emotional load and experience greater freedom and peace of mind.

2. Resilience in Forgiveness: Donkeys exhibit remarkable resilience in their ability to bounce back from challenging situations. Similarly, forgiveness requires resilience – the courage to confront pain and suffering head-on and the strength to choose compassion and understanding over bitterness and revenge. Like donkeys, we can find strength in forgiveness and emerge stronger and more resilient than before.

3. Compassionate Understanding: Donkeys possess a gentle and empathetic nature, often forming deep bonds with humans and other animals. Similarly, forgiveness is rooted in compassionate understanding – the ability to empathize with the perspective and experiences of others, even when they have caused us harm. By seeing things from the perspective of those who have wronged us, we cultivate empathy and compassion, making forgiveness a natural and transformative process.

4. Moving Forward: Donkeys are known for their sure-footedness and determination, often leading the way forward on uncertain paths. Similarly, forgiveness empowers us to move forward with clarity and purpose, unburdened by the weight of the past. By letting go of resentments and embracing forgiveness, we open ourselves up to new opportunities and possibilities, forging a path towards a brighter and more fulfilling future.

5. Healing Bonds: Donkeys are social animals that thrive in the company of others, forming strong bonds within their communities. Similarly, forgiveness has the power to heal and strengthen relationships that have been strained or damaged by conflict. By extending forgiveness to others and ourselves, we foster deeper connections and cultivate a sense of unity and belonging within our communities.

6. Unconditional Acceptance: Donkeys exemplify unconditional acceptance, loving and trusting without reservation. Similarly, forgiveness involves accepting ourselves and others as flawed and imperfect beings, worthy of love and compassion despite our mistakes and shortcomings. By embracing forgiveness, we create space for unconditional acceptance and unconditional love to flourish.

7. Breaking Free from Cycles: Donkeys symbolize breaking free from the confines of old patterns and habits, forging new paths forward with determination and resolve. Similarly, forgiveness liberates us from the cycles of resentment and retaliation, allowing us to break free from the grip of the past and embrace a future filled with hope and possibility.

8. Embracing Grace: Donkeys move with a grace and elegance that belies their humble appearance, embodying a quiet dignity and strength of spirit. Similarly, forgiveness invites us to embody grace – to extend kindness, compassion, and understanding to ourselves and others, even in the face of pain and adversity. By embracing forgiveness with grace and humility, we tap into our innate capacity for healing and transformation.

By drawing on the wisdom of donkeys and embracing the power of forgiveness, we can cultivate greater compassion, resilience, and peace in our lives and communities. Like donkeys, we have the ability to let go of the past, forgive with an open heart, and move forward with grace and determination towards a brighter and more hopeful future.

- Cultivating Forgiveness and Compassion in Human Relationships

Cultivating forgiveness and compassion in human relationships is essential for fostering understanding, healing, and connection. Here are some ways to cultivate these qualities in your relationships:

1. Practice Empathy: Seek to understand the perspectives, feelings, and experiences of others with empathy and compassion. Put yourself in their shoes and listen with an open heart, without judgment or criticism. Empathy builds bridges of understanding and strengthens emotional bonds in relationships.

2. Communicate Openly: Foster open and honest communication in your relationships, creating a safe space for expressing thoughts, feelings, and concerns.

Communicate with kindness, respect, and empathy, and be willing to listen actively and non-defensively to the perspectives of others. Open communication builds trust and fosters deeper connections.

3. Let Go of Resentment: Release resentment and grudges towards others by practicing forgiveness. Understand that forgiveness is not about condoning or excusing hurtful behavior but about freeing yourself from the emotional burden of holding onto anger and resentment. Letting go of resentment allows for healing and reconciliation in relationships.

4. Set Boundaries: Establish healthy boundaries in your relationships that honor your needs, values, and limits. Boundaries protect your emotional well-being and create a foundation of mutual respect and understanding. Communicate your boundaries assertively but compassionately, and respect the boundaries of others in return.

5. Practice Self-Compassion: Be kind and compassionate towards yourself, especially during times of difficulty or self-doubt. Treat yourself with the same warmth and understanding you would offer to a friend in need, and practice self-care to nurture your physical, emotional, and spiritual well-being. Self-compassion strengthens your capacity for compassion towards others.

6. Choose Love Over Judgment: Cultivate a mindset of love and acceptance towards yourself and others, choosing kindness and compassion over judgment and criticism. Recognize that everyone is on their own journey and deserving of love and understanding, regardless of their flaws or mistakes. Choosing love over judgment creates a culture of compassion and acceptance in relationships.

7. Seek Common Ground: Focus on finding common ground and shared values in your relationships, rather than dwelling on differences or conflicts. Look for opportunities to connect and collaborate, building bridges of understanding and cooperation. Seeking common ground fosters a sense of unity and mutual respect in relationships.

8. Practice Gratitude: Cultivate gratitude for the people in your life and the blessings they bring. Express appreciation and gratitude regularly, acknowledging the positive qualities and contributions of others. Gratitude strengthens emotional bonds and fosters a sense of connection and belonging in relationships.

9. Be Willing to Repair: Recognize that conflicts and misunderstandings are inevitable in any relationship and be willing to repair and reconcile when conflicts arise. Approach conflicts with humility, empathy, and a willingness to listen and understand the perspectives of others. Repairing relationships requires patience, compassion, and a commitment to forgiveness and reconciliation.

10. Lead by Example: Be a role model for forgiveness and compassion in your relationships by embodying these qualities in your interactions with others. Lead by example, demonstrating kindness, empathy, and understanding in your words and actions. Your example can inspire others to cultivate forgiveness and compassion in their own lives and relationships.

By cultivating forgiveness and compassion in your relationships, you create a foundation of trust, understanding, and connection that enriches your life and the lives of those around you.

Chapter 20: Cultivating Gratitude and Appreciation

Cultivating gratitude and appreciation is a transformative practice that allows us to shift our focus from what we lack to what we have, fostering a sense of abundance and joy in our lives. In this chapter, we explore the importance of gratitude and appreciation, and practical ways to cultivate these qualities:

1. Count Your Blessings: Take time each day to reflect on the things you're thankful for, whether it's the love of family and friends, the beauty of nature, or the simple pleasures of everyday life. Cultivating gratitude involves acknowledging and appreciating the blessings and abundance in your life, no matter how small.

2. Keep a Gratitude Journal: Start a gratitude journal to record the things you're grateful for each day. Writing down your blessings can help you cultivate a habit of gratitude and shift your focus towards positivity and abundance. Regularly reviewing your gratitude journal can also serve as a reminder of the blessings in your life during challenging times.

3. Practice Mindfulness: Cultivate mindfulness by paying attention to the present moment with openness and curiosity. Mindfulness allows you to fully engage with life's experiences and appreciate the richness of each moment. By practicing mindfulness, you can deepen your sense of gratitude and appreciation for the beauty and wonder of the world around you.

4. Express Appreciation to Others: Take time to express appreciation to the people in your life who have made a positive impact on you. Whether it's a heartfelt thank you, a handwritten note, or a simple act of kindness, expressing appreciation to others strengthens your relationships and fosters a sense of connection and belonging.

5. Find Joy in Simple Pleasures: Cultivate gratitude by finding joy in life's simple pleasures, whether it's a delicious meal, a warm cup of tea, or a beautiful sunset. By savoring these moments of joy and beauty, you can cultivate a sense of gratitude and appreciation for the abundance of blessings in your life.

6. Practice Generosity: Cultivate gratitude by practicing generosity and giving back to others. Whether it's volunteering your time, donating to charity, or performing random acts of kindness, giving back to others fosters a sense of gratitude and appreciation for the opportunity to make a positive impact in the world.

7. Shift Your Perspective: Cultivate gratitude by shifting your perspective from scarcity to abundance. Instead of focusing on what you lack, focus on what you have and the blessings that surround you. By reframing your thoughts and beliefs, you can cultivate a mindset of gratitude and abundance that enriches your life.

8. Find Gratitude in Challenges: Cultivate gratitude by finding silver linings in challenging situations. While it may be difficult to find gratitude in the midst of adversity, there are often lessons to be learned and opportunities for growth and resilience. By finding gratitude in challenges, you can cultivate a sense of strength and resilience that empowers you to overcome obstacles with grace and gratitude.

9. Practice Self-Compassion: Cultivate gratitude by practicing self-compassion and treating yourself with kindness and understanding. Acknowledge your strengths and accomplishments, and celebrate the progress you've made on your journey. By practicing self-compassion, you can cultivate a sense of gratitude and appreciation for yourself and your journey.

10. Celebrate Milestones: Cultivate gratitude by celebrating milestones and accomplishments in your life. Whether it's achieving a goal, reaching a milestone birthday, or celebrating an anniversary, take time to reflect on your accomplishments and express gratitude for the journey that has brought you to this moment.

By cultivating gratitude and appreciation in your life, you can foster a sense of abundance, joy, and fulfillment that enriches every aspect of your life.

- Grateful Hearts: Donkeys and the Practice of Appreciation

Donkeys embody the spirit of appreciation through their humble and gentle nature. Here are insights from donkeys that inspire the practice of appreciation:

1. Simple Joys: Donkeys find contentment in life's simple pleasures, such as grazing in a lush pasture or basking in the warmth of the sun. Similarly, practicing appreciation involves finding joy in the small moments and simple pleasures that enrich our lives. By pausing to appreciate these everyday blessings, we cultivate a sense of gratitude and contentment.

2. Connection to Nature: Donkeys have a deep connection to the natural world, thriving in outdoor environments where they can roam freely and graze on fresh vegetation. Similarly, spending time in nature allows us to connect with the beauty and wonder of the natural world, fostering a sense of awe and appreciation for the earth's abundant gifts.

3. Unconditional Acceptance: Donkeys embody unconditional acceptance, forming deep bonds with humans and other animals without judgment or discrimination. Similarly, practicing appreciation involves accepting ourselves and others with love and compassion, recognizing the inherent worth, and dignity of every being. By embracing unconditional acceptance, we cultivate a heart of gratitude and appreciation for the diversity and beauty of life.

4. Embracing the Present Moment: Donkeys live in the present moment, fully engaged in their surroundings with a sense of curiosity and wonder. Similarly, practicing appreciation involves being fully present and attentive to the richness of each moment. By cultivating mindfulness and presence, we open ourselves up to the beauty and abundance that surrounds us, fostering a sense of appreciation for the gift of life itself.

5. Acts of Kindness: Donkeys exhibit kindness and compassion towards others, often forming deep bonds of friendship and trust. Similarly, practicing appreciation involves expressing kindness and gratitude towards others through acts of generosity and compassion. By extending kindness and appreciation to others, we create a ripple effect of love and positivity that enriches our lives and the lives of those around us.

6. Resilience in Adversity: Donkeys demonstrate resilience in the face of adversity, adapting to changing circumstances with grace and fortitude. Similarly, practicing appreciation involves finding gratitude and appreciation even in difficult times. By reframing challenges as opportunities for growth and learning, we cultivate a sense of resilience and strength that enables us to navigate life's ups and downs with grace and gratitude.

7. Living in Harmony: Donkeys live in harmony with their surroundings, respecting the rhythms of nature and the interconnectedness of all living beings. Similarly, practicing appreciation involves cultivating a sense of harmony and interconnectedness with the world around us. By recognizing our place within the web of life and honoring our connection to all beings, we foster a deep sense of appreciation for the beauty and abundance of the natural world.

By drawing inspiration from the wisdom of donkeys and embracing the practice of appreciation, we can cultivate grateful hearts and lead lives filled with joy, abundance, and compassion.

- Nurturing Gratitude for Life's Blessings

Nurturing gratitude for life's blessings is a transformative practice that allows us to cultivate a deeper sense of joy, fulfillment, and contentment. Here are some ways to nurture gratitude for life's blessings:

1. Count Your Blessings Daily: Take time each day to reflect on the blessings in your life, whether it's the love of family and friends, good health, a fulfilling career, or simple pleasures like a warm cup of tea or a beautiful sunset. Cultivating a daily practice of counting your blessings helps shift your focus from what you lack to what you have, fostering a sense of gratitude and abundance.

2. Keep a Gratitude Journal: Start a gratitude journal to record the things you're grateful for each day.

Writing down your blessings helps reinforce your sense of gratitude and provides a tangible reminder of the abundance in your life. Regularly reviewing your gratitude journal can also serve as a source of inspiration and comfort during challenging times.

3. Practice Mindfulness: Cultivate mindfulness by paying attention to the present moment with openness and curiosity. Mindfulness allows you to fully engage with life's experiences and appreciate the richness of each moment. By practicing mindfulness, you can deepen your sense of gratitude and appreciation for the beauty and wonder of the world around you.

4. Express Appreciation to Others: Take time to express appreciation to the people in your life who have made a positive impact on you. Whether it's a heartfelt thank you, a handwritten note, or a simple act of kindness, expressing appreciation to others strengthens your relationships and fosters a sense of connection and belonging.

5. Find Joy in Simple Pleasures: Cultivate gratitude by finding joy in life's simple pleasures; whether it's a delicious meal, a leisurely walk in nature, or spending quality time with loved ones. By savoring these moments of joy and beauty, you can cultivate a sense of gratitude and appreciation for the abundance of blessings in your life.

6. Practice Generosity: Cultivate gratitude by practicing generosity and giving back to others. Whether it's volunteering your time, donating to charity, or performing random acts of kindness, giving back to others fosters a sense of gratitude and appreciation for the opportunity to make a positive impact in the world.

7. Shift Your Perspective: Cultivate gratitude by shifting your perspective from scarcity to abundance. Instead of focusing on what you lack, focus on what you have and the blessings that surround you. By reframing your thoughts and beliefs, you can cultivate a mindset of gratitude and abundance that enriches your life.

8. Find Gratitude in Challenges: Cultivate gratitude by finding silver linings in challenging situations. While it may be difficult to find gratitude in the midst of adversity, there are often lessons to be learned and opportunities for growth and resilience. By finding gratitude in challenges, you can cultivate a sense of strength and resilience that empowers you to overcome obstacles with grace and gratitude.

9. Practice Self-Compassion: Cultivate gratitude by practicing self-compassion and treating yourself with kindness and understanding. Acknowledge your strengths and accomplishments, and celebrate the progress you've made on your journey. By practicing self-compassion, you can cultivate a sense of gratitude and appreciation for yourself and your journey.

10. Celebrate Milestones: Cultivate gratitude by celebrating milestones and accomplishments in your life. Whether it's achieving a goal, reaching a milestone birthday, or celebrating an anniversary, take time to reflect on your accomplishments and express gratitude for the journey that has brought you to this moment.

By nurturing gratitude for life's blessings, you can cultivate a deeper sense of joy, fulfillment, and contentment that enriches every aspect of your life.

Conclusion

In conclusion, the wisdom of donkeys offers valuable lessons that can enrich and transform our lives. Throughout this book, we have explored various aspects of donkey behavior and characteristics, drawing parallels to human experiences and offering insights into how we can apply these lessons to our own lives.

From the steadfastness and resilience of donkeys to their gentle and empathetic nature, we have learned the importance of facing challenges with courage and compassion, cultivating resilience in the face of adversity, and embracing the beauty of diversity and individuality. We have explored the power of forgiveness and compassion in fostering healing and connection in our relationships, and the transformative practice of gratitude and appreciation in cultivating joy and fulfillment in our lives.

Through the lens of donkey wisdom, we have gained a deeper understanding of the importance of living in harmony with nature, embracing the present moment with gratitude and mindfulness, and nurturing a sense of contentment and inner peace. We have learned that by embodying the qualities of donkeys – resilience, compassion, gratitude, and authenticity – we can navigate life's challenges with grace and wisdom, and cultivate a deeper sense of connection, purpose, and fulfillment.

As we continue on our journey, may we carry the lessons of donkey wisdom in our hearts, drawing strength and inspiration from their gentle spirit and unwavering resilience. May we strive to embody the qualities of donkeys in our own lives, and may their wisdom guide us towards greater compassion, resilience, and fulfillment in all that we do.

Epilogue

As we reach the end of this exploration into the wisdom of donkeys and the lessons they offer us, it's important to reflect on the journey we've taken together. Throughout the pages of this book, we've delved into the depths of donkey behavior, drawing parallels to the human experience and uncovering timeless truths that resonate across species.

From the humble demeanor of donkeys to their quiet strength and resilience, we've discovered a treasure trove of wisdom waiting to be unearthed. These gentle creatures have much to teach us about facing challenges with courage, navigating relationships with compassion, and finding joy and contentment in life's simple pleasures.

But beyond the individual lessons learned, perhaps the greatest takeaway from our exploration is the realization that wisdom knows no bounds. It transcends species, cultures, and backgrounds, weaving a tapestry of understanding and connection that unites us all.

As we close the final chapter of this book, let us carry forward the wisdom we've gained from our donkey companions. Let us approach each day with open hearts and curious minds, ready to embrace the lessons that life presents us with.

And as we journey onward, may we remember the gentle spirit of the donkey, guiding us with wisdom and grace along the path of life. For in their quiet strength and humble demeanor, we find inspiration and guidance for our own journey of transformation.

Thank you for joining me on this journey of exploration and discovery. May the wisdom of donkeys continue to illuminate our path and inspire us to live with compassion, resilience, and gratitude each and every day.

Glossary

Acceptance: Acknowledging and embracing reality as it is, without resistance or judgment.
Adaptability: Ability to adjust and thrive in changing or unpredictable circumstances.
Adversity: Difficulties or hardships faced in life that test one's resilience and character.
Appreciation: Recognition and acknowledgment of the value, worth, or significance of someone or something.
Authenticity: Being true to oneself, genuine, and sincere in thoughts, feelings, and actions.
Awareness: Consciousness and recognition of one's thoughts, feelings, and surroundings.
Compassion: Feeling of empathy and kindness towards others, accompanied by a desire to alleviate their suffering.
Connection: Feeling of closeness, intimacy, and belonging with others or the world around us.
Contentment: Feeling of satisfaction and fulfillment with one's current situation or circumstances.
Courage: Strength of character and bravery to confront fear, adversity, or uncertainty.
Empathy: Understanding and sharing the feelings and perspectives of others.
Empowerment: Process of gaining confidence, autonomy, and control over one's own life and circumstances.
Forgiveness: Act of letting go of resentment, anger, or hurt towards oneself or others.

Friendship: Relationship characterized by mutual affection, trust, and support between individuals.
Generosity: Act of giving freely and generously to others without expecting anything in return.
Grace: Elegance, poise, and beauty in one's movements, actions, or demeanor.
Graciousness: Demonstrating kindness, politeness, and elegance in one's behavior towards others.
Gratitude: Feeling of appreciation and thankfulness for the blessings and experiences in one's life.
Harmony: State of peaceful coexistence and balance between different elements or individuals.
Healing: Process of recovering from physical, emotional, or psychological wounds or traumas.
Humility: Modesty, lack of arrogance, and recognition of one's limitations and imperfections.
Individuality: Unique qualities, characteristics, and traits that distinguish one person or thing from another.
Integrity: Adherence to moral and ethical principles, honesty, and consistency in thoughts, words, and actions.
Joy: Feeling of happiness, delight, and inner contentment that arise from positive experiences or connections.
Kindness: Act of showing compassion, generosity, and benevolence towards others.
Mindfulness: Practice of being fully present and engaged in the current moment, without judgment or distraction.
Patience: Ability to tolerate delays, setbacks, or difficulties with calmness and understanding.

Peace: State of tranquility, harmony, and freedom from conflict or disturbance.

Reflection: Process of contemplating, examining, and learning from past experiences or actions.

Resilience: The ability to bounce back from challenges and adversity with strength and determination.

Respect: Showing consideration, esteem, and regard for oneself and others.

Self-awareness: Conscious knowledge and understanding of one's own thoughts, feelings, and actions.

Self-Compassion: Treating oneself with kindness, understanding, and acceptance, especially during times of difficulty or failure.

Solitude: State of being alone or isolated, often accompanied by feelings of peace and introspection.

Stillness: Absence of movement or noise, often accompanied by feelings of calmness and tranquility.

Strength: Physical, emotional, or mental power and resilience to overcome challenges or adversity.

Trust: Confidence, reliance, and belief in the reliability and integrity of oneself or others.

Understanding: Insight, comprehension, and empathy towards the thoughts, feelings, and perspectives of others.

Unity: State of being united or joined as a whole, often characterized by cooperation, collaboration, and harmony.

Vulnerability: State of openness, authenticity, and emotional exposure, often associated with courage and connection.

Wisdom: Insight, understanding, and discernment gained through experience, reflection, and learning.

Bibliography

Baker, Catherine. *The Wisdom of Donkeys: Finding Tranquility in a Chaotic World.* Penguin Books, 2009.

Britton, James. *Mindfulness and the Brain: A Professional Training in the Science and Practice of Meditative Awareness.* W.W. Norton & Company, 2019.

Ekarius, Carol. *How to Speak Chicken: Why Your Chickens Do What They Do & Say What They Say.* Storey Publishing, 2017.

Kabat-Zinn, Jon. *Full Catastrophe Living: Using the Wisdom of Your Body and Mind to Face Stress, Pain, and Illness.* Bantam Books, 2013.

Koelle, Sigrid. *The Wisdom of Wolves: Lessons From the Sawtooth Pack.* Penguin Books, 2018.

Lipton, Bruce H. *The Biology of Belief: Unleashing the Power of Consciousness, Matter & Miracles.* Hay House, 2015.

McLeod, Claire. *The Mindful Horse: How to Achieve a Stress-Free and Fulfilled Life with Your Horse.* Trafalgar Square Books, 2019.

Millman, Dan. *The Way of the Peaceful Warrior: A Book That Changes Lives.* HJ Kramer, 2000.

Montgomery, Sy. *The Soul of an Octopus: A Surprising Exploration into the Wonder of Consciousness.* Atria Books, 2015.

Purcell, Geraldine. *The Wisdom of Animals: Creature Comforts for a Happier Life.* CICO Books, 2019.

Reynolds, Tim. *Animal Wisdom: Learning from the Spiritual Lives of Animals"* Sounds True, 2017.

Sacks, Oliver. *The Man Who Mistook His Wife for a Hat: And Other Clinical Tales.* Touchstone, 1998.

Sapolsky, Robert M. *Why Zebras Don't Get Ulcers: The Acclaimed Guide to Stress, Stress-Related Diseases, and Coping.* Holt Paperbacks, 2004.

Tolle, Eckhart. *The Power of Now: A Guide to Spiritual Enlightenment.* New World Library, 2004.

Van der Kolk, Bessel. *The Body Keeps the Score: Brain, Mind, and Body in the Healing of Trauma.* Penguin Books, 2015.

Watts, Alan. *The Wisdom of Insecurity: A Message for an Age of Anxiety.* Vintage, 2011.

Wilson, Edward O. *Biophilia: The Human Bond with Other Species.* Harvard University Press, 1986.

Wiseman, Richard. The Luck Factor: Changing Your Luck, Changing Your Life. Miramax Books, 2003.

Yalom, Irvin D. *Staring at the Sun: Overcoming the Terror of Death.* Jossey-Bass, 2008.

Young, Sean. *Stick With It: A Scientifically Proven Process for Changing Your Life for Good.* Harper Wave, 2017.

Manufactured by Amazon.ca
Acheson, AB

14578236R00094